# Islam and the Challenge of Civilization

# Islam and the Challenge of Civilization

ABDELWAHAB MEDDEB

*Translated by Jane Kuntz*

FORDHAM UNIVERSITY PRESS

*New York* 2013

Copyright © 2013 Fordham University Press

All rights reserved. No part of this publication may be
reproduced, stored in a retrieval system, or transmitted in
any form or by any means—electronic, mechanical,
photocopy, recording, or any other—except for brief
quotations in printed reviews, without the prior permission
of the publisher.

This work was originally published in French as *Pari de
civilisation*, © Éditions du Seuil, 2009.

Cet ouvrage a bénéficié du soutien des Programmes d'aide à
la publication de l'Institut Français.

This work, published as part of a program of aid for
publication, received support from the Institut Français.

Ouvrage publié avec le concours du Ministère français
chargé de la Culture–Centre National du Livre.

This work has been published with the assistance of the
French Ministry of Culture–National Center for the Book.

Fordham University Press has no responsibility for the
persistence or accuracy of URLs for external or third-party
Internet websites referred to in this publication and does not
guarantee that any content on such websites is, or will
remain, accurate or appropriate.

Fordham University Press also publishes its books in a
variety of electronic formats. Some content that appears in
print may not be available in electronic books.

Library of Congress Cataloging-in-Publication Data is
available from the publisher.

Printed in the United States of America

15  14  13    5  4  3  2  1

First edition

# Contents

## Prologue:   Religion and Violence

All is not well with Islam. In fact, it is seriously ailing. I have ventured to diagnose this ailment and to prescribe the cure in four previous books written since the horrendous attacks of September 11, 2001.[1] This new work is an extension of the scrutiny undertaken in those earlier ones. I open with a reminder that this ailment can be best summed up as the use of violence in the name of God. I will pursue this point of inquiry, asking whether it is somehow a fate peculiar to Islam, or whether we are dealing here with a structural feature shared by religious constructions in general.

I posit from the outset that violence produced by belief is not unique to Islam but finds virulent expression even among beliefs issuing from the Indian subcontinent, a region stereotypically associated with a spirituality grounded in the miracle of nonviolence. Thus, an apparent predisposition to violence is in evidence beyond the sphere of monotheisms, whose internal conflict, need I point out, is itself fratricidal by nature.

One has only to survey monotheisms over space and time to note that wars fought in the name of the Lord were biblical before they were Koranic. One typical illustration would be the massacre ordered by an angry Moses upon discovering that his people had lapsed into paganism. As a result of the Golden Calf episode, the Levites carried out the orders of their prophet and slaughtered three thousand people in one day (Exodus 32:28). Joshua, successor to the founder, was no exception. If readers need convincing, I would urge them to reread the passage relating to the massacre he perpetrated after the fall of Jericho, where he spared neither man, woman, nor child, nor even animals (Joshua 6:21). Today, certain fanatical Jewish literalists are seeking to universalize and contemporize what they call the Judgment of Amalek, which refers to the chief of the Amalekites, whom the Hebrews had to combat, because they were preventing the Hebrews from getting to the Promised Land (Exodus 17:8–15).

Thus, when it comes to violence, the Prophet of Islam is a direct descendant of the Old Testament. The much-discussed "Verse of the Sword" ordaining that pagans be killed and the "War Verse" calling for a fight to the death against Christians and Jews both have a "biblical" ring (Koran 9:5, 29). Yet it is these verses that feed the murderous fanaticism of fundamentalist Muslims.

If the exercise of violence seems consistent with revealed scripture, nevertheless an important matter of degree distinguishes Judaism from Islam, which is that the latter universalizes what the former particularizes. Where Judaism wages the Lord's war for the Holy Land only, Islam sets its sights on the entire world. Contemporary Muslim fundamentalists did not invent *jihād*, the driving force that propelled the expansion of Islam from the start. As an eleventh-century Chinese chronicler, Ou-Yang Hsui, attests, Muslim troops hurled themselves into the thick of battle, hoping for martyrdom, after their chief had galvanized them with promises of paradise for those who die in combat for the holy cause.[2]

Though it is true that the Gospels move away from this violence, Christians have nonetheless resorted to surprising extremes of violence over the course of history. I see in this a betrayal of Christianity's founding message. Admittedly, Augustine theorized the just war to defend the city against barbarian invasion. He was not talking about a call to war in the name of the faith, but the Doctor of Hippo had to legitimize that call even though he knew it conflicted with the spirit of the Gospels. The notion of a just war has often been contested in Christian circles, where it is considered to be in direct contradiction with Christ's teachings. Hence, to justify the use of violence, the notion of necessary war was introduced. Yet it took nearly a millennium and the launching of the Crusades for Christianity to arrive at a notion equivalent to *jihād*, perhaps to counter its effects using the same weapons.

These reminders are not intended to mitigate the malady that is afflicting Islam, but to show that believers often take their founding scriptures a step further, or even move beyond them altogether. If, throughout history, Christianity has not always honored the Gospel's message of peace, Islam today should still strive to find a way to foil those clauses of the Koranic text that call for war. This book works toward that goal by waging what I call the war of interpretations, while placing special emphasis on the context in which the holy text itself was issued and received.

This check on violence via the return to context is absolutely crucial, with regard not only to the question of violence but also to the many anthropological anachronisms carried forward by the law that issues from the spirit and the letter of the founding text (here, of course, I am thinking of the Koran-inspired *sharīʿa*).

Again, with regard to violence, states founded in Islam will need to realize that it is their duty to counteract the notion of holy war, of *jihād*, for it flagrantly contradicts both their participation in the concert of nations and the march toward the Kantian utopia of "perpetual peace" that has remained an aspiration of the times, despite the persistence of war and the hegemonic effects of the powerful, with their urge to rule the world. Indeed, an ever more diverse sample of humanity is trending toward hegemony by force of arms or economic clout. Is this not the aim of emerging nations such as China, India, and the Arab oil states alongside Europe and the United States?

Islamic countries must wake up to the fact that times have changed, that the world is a different place. When it comes to religious identity, Islam continues to perceive Christianity as if it were still its medieval antagonist, despite modern notions of nation and peoples that have circumscribed the influence of religion. And now that the whole issue of state has become postnational, the factor of religion is receding even further. In Europe, for example, religion necessarily cedes priority to the all-important prime notion of citizenship, one that involves a wholly different set of laws designed outside the kind of religious prescription that belongs to another age.

In short, if Islam is to be cured of its current affliction, it must get to that post-Islamic, postreligious place where Christianity and Judaism have managed to arrive. Only this will ease the tension that prevails among nations. But for the moment, the Islamic states—Saudi Arabia in particular—exhort their citizenry to practice a middle-of-the-road Islam, with the intention of setting them off from their fellow Muslims who live their faith according to a more extreme, maximalist interpretation. These moderates base their appeal theologically on the Koran, which refers negatively to these extremists as *ghulw*, calling for moderation among all the "People of the Book" in interpreting their respective dogmas (Koran 4:171, 5:77).

This is a praiseworthy step, though woefully inadequate and timid, especially when it comes to the presence of Islam in Europe. Here, we have the means to achieve an operative post-Islamic space by urging the Muslim citizens of Europe to live according to their free conscience, in the spirit of positive law and the charter of human rights, abolishing any reference to *shariʿa*. As such, these Muslims who make their own free choices will be practicing a more spiritualized, less legalistic worship that will draw on the mystical side of their religious tradition, the rich Sufi substratum to which I often refer in the pages that follow.

In this book, I propose a series of rereadings of the founding text and the Tradition (*sunna* and *hadīth*) to conduct this effort to neutralize and move beyond religion. This will result in a transfiguration of values achieved through an enhanced familiarity with Islamic material, not by merely glossing it or neglecting it altogether. It is by revisiting the Islamic past, by focusing on those aspects that moved civilization forward, that we will recover the means to get beyond the restrictive boundaries of identity and become active participants on the world scene, in full acknowledgment of who we once were and who we have become. In other words, the politics and poetics of the effort to neutralize and surpass cannot be effective without a fresh redeployment of the founding reference, one that inscribes Islam anew rather than suppressing or ignoring it. It is not in denial but rather in full recognition of the Islamic self that Islam's believers will gain access to the cosmopolitan stage and will turn away from barbarity and make their contribution to contemporary world civilization. This is the challenge of civilization that I will be putting forth.

But first, believers must be freed from their worship of scripture, with its literal reading and one-track interpretation, which can only lead to violence. Next, meaning derived from the text must be placed back in the context from which it issued: I will do this at every opportunity. To carry out such a project, one has to make the Koran one's own, to renew the energy it inspires by becoming Koran oneself, as if at the time of its reception, playing the role in the presence of the angel, as recommended by Ibn 'Arabī, who never ceased repeating throughout his works: "Be Koran unto yourself" (*kun qur'ān fī nafsika*). This initiative will have us experience the Koran as myth, but will not prevent us from situating it within its historical moment in order to wage the necessary hermeneutic battle and restore to the Text its myriad of meanings out of the deafening clash of interpretations.

*Your cure is within you, but you are not aware*
*And your illness comes from within, but you see it not.*

   —Molla Sadra

*The cure for the disease within the disease itself*

   —Jean-Jacques Rousseau

# CHAPTER I

# The Koran as Myth

I

My relationship to Arabic, particularly Koranic Arabic, is at the core of who I am as a person. As a child, my experience of Arabic diglossia was a very physical one. My mother tongue was the Tunis vulgate, used by my mother and the women in my family home. Next, at the age of four, I was inducted into what I will call the "father tongue," a notion I borrow from Dante and his relation to Virgil, his father figure and guide in the first two parts of the *Divine Comedy*. Dante's father tongue was Latin, regulated by "grammar," as distinct from the "vulgate," as he said, "which we speak without rules, imitating our nurse,"[1] and which would be reinvented by the Tuscan poet once he had chosen it as his writing language. For me, the father tongue was the Arabic of the Koran, very different from the dialect, and which dates from the late seventh and early eighth centuries, an archaic idiom comparable to other dead languages that linger in the collective memory. Though one will hear anecdotally that Arabic has not changed much, there is no denying that it has actually evolved considerably. When linguists broach the topic, they speak of a language locked in time, but this fixedness is relative, for the language has undergone very deep changes, despite appearances. This ambivalence between dead or living language is what makes Arabic such an effective liturgical medium. So, at the age of four, when I was first introduced to the Koran by my father, that language began working with my mother tongue in a system of communicating vessels. My father was a theologian, an *'alīm*, a member of that last generation of traditional doctors of religion that made up the faculty of the mosque-based university of the Zaytūna (founded in the ninth century). He was thus my initiator in the full sense of the term, both for the Koran and for its language.

To this first literacy training via the Koran was added modern schooling at age six when I was enrolled in a bilingual primary school (Arabic and French). The foreign language then clustered with the other two. It would be incidental here to dwell on all the benefits of this third language (which could be called a vehicle, a language of knowledge as power) in terms of complexity, tension, situations of linguistic complicity and competition, and blurring of boundaries, none of which impeded the mutual contamination, the creation of hybrids and even creoles.

From that point forward, traditional education no longer exercised an exclusive claim on my learning time. Yet I was able to gain an insider's perspective on the impact of this paternal decision to see that I was exposed to the Koran as material for learning to read, write, and recite. This early apprenticeship via the Koran granted a privileged status to the father tongue. From a tender age, then, young Muslims internalize the notion that the sacred language is the language of the Father, the language through which the Law is transmitted, keeping alive the genealogical principle from elder master to young initiate. This transmission is all the more effective in that, for a child catechumen, the language of initiation remains obscure, steeped in a kind of hieratic majesty that distances without separating entirely from the mother tongue, the vernacular that provides the speaker with his or her first tools of communication. I learned the Koran by heart, understanding virtually nothing. But at the same time, I did recognize phrases, words here and there, the same we used in everyday speech. My learning of the Koran came to resemble a walk through a dark forest with occasional clearings, nevertheless, where shafts of light shone on scattered bits of meaning.

This early contact with Koranic language endowed me with a penchant for what I call poetic reading. I favored a physical rapport with language, whichever one it might be. I was attentive to its scansion, to the way the combination of vowels and consonants produced a musicality. I yielded to the overwhelming desire to return the text before my eyes to its oral origins, as if sound evinced sense. Whether voiced or graphically represented, a language acquires a holy status when the signifier takes precedence over the signified.

2

This personal experience testifies to something universal in Islam. The same principle is at work where the theory and practice of Koranic psalmody (*tajwīd*) is concerned. The technique involved in this chanted reading is based on the construction of musical forms that exalt sound, thereby impeding access to meaning. In other words, the privilege granted to sound suppresses other forms of reception by inciting the cantor to improvise, to test harmonic patterns and rhythms that play on the effects produced by contraction and expansion, lengthening and shortening, staccato and legato, the dense and the ethereal, compact and airy, pushing vocal capacities to the limit of how they might act upon the column of air breathed in and out in an intensely disciplined and studied manner. The text is thus overwhelmed by a halo of chant whereby the melodic undulations that deliver word and phrase end up diverting

attention away from syntax and meaning. The effort to produce
the most exalted sound determines the diction, sometimes at
the expense of grammatical and phonological logic, and ob-
scures the syntactical patterns.

This withdrawal of meaning, this emphasis placed upon the
signifier at the expense of the signified, is also present in visual
systems of representation where the material object represented
is the written word of the Koran. This is particularly noticeable
in the move from mere inscription to decorative calligraphy
within the codex, a shift marked by an aesthetic intent that
gets magnified when the letter migrates from the page to cover
all available surfaces, from solid objects to textiles to walls. By
virtue of this migration and its underlying theory, calligraphy
rose to the top rank in the hierarchy of visual arts. Once in-
stalled in the monumental order, the letter enters the vocabulary of architecture: despite its two-dimensionality, it stands
out from the wall and occupies three-dimensional space. This
spatial presence of letters suspends the reading process, as if
making sense of the written word were no longer the main
purpose of its deployment. Calligraphy thus constitutes a fine
example of the role played by prior knowledge (*ma'arifa*), which
acts as a potent aid to our power of discrimination (*al-quwwa
al-ma'āni*), a reading skill that is facilitated whenever one recalls having already seen the bit of text in question, a function
of memory (*dhākir*), in other words. This mental operation will
increase the stock of "familiarized meanings" (*al-ma'āni al-
ma'lūfa*) that a subject will draw upon as he or she observes the
world and all that dwells there.[2] Confronted with the obstacle
of graphic style that transforms the letters' legibility, observers
manage to recover the chain of meaning only when they reconstitute memorized verses by identifying a word here and there
that will eventually lead them to restore the sentence to the
appropriate *sūrat*. This act of deciphering cannot take place
without the eye first triggering an act of recognition of what
the reader already knows.

The visual spectacle of calligraphy is meant to reveal its musical origins. In the encyclopedia of the Brothers of Purity (tenth century),[3] calligraphy as an art form is addressed in the epistle devoted to music, the fifth, itself belonging to the part comprising the mathematical sciences (*riyāzīyāt*). Calligraphy, like music, is perceived as an art deriving from mathematics or, more precisely, geometry, an art based on ratio and proportion, and as such a middle ground between abstraction and anatomical representation in painting and sculpture.

Thus, aside from voice alone, the Koranic letter is sublimated by another form of musicality, a further form of exaltation underpinned by the graphic aspect. It is as if, in both cases (psalmody and calligraphy), the relation to the text necessarily recalls the primal scene where the child discovers strange echoes between the Father language and the Mother tongue; as if the voice of God were reaching the ears of the living via the language of the dead that maintains a viable form, audible to ears receptive to this dialogue, though leaving the meaning unresolved. Of course, this situation loses its subtlety when the mother tongue of the catechumen falls outside the sphere of Arabic dialects. Whenever Koranic initiation moves from the diglossic to the bilingual (speakers of Tachelhit, Wolof, Swahili, Turkish, Persian, Sogdian, Urdu, Hindi, Chinese, Bosnian, etc.) the reception of Koranic language shifts from strange familiarity to face a more radical strangeness.

3

To this initial encoding, we can add a further sanctification via the fiction purporting that the Koran transcribes the uncreated word of God. Thanks to this myth, a human language is rendered divine. Beyond the predominance acquired by the language of the Koran by way of its traditional pedagogical method, its place in the collective consciousness has been enhanced by this myth, making it for all eternity the instrument of the absolute, the infinite, the unknowable, the invisible. The dogma of *i'jāz* confirms this holy and inviolate nature by declaring humans powerless to solve the Mystery involved in the linguistic performance of the Koran, considered miraculous in and of itself. Orientalists translate the term *i'jāz* as the "unsurpassable" or "inimitable and wondrous" nature of the Koran,[4] a translation that evades the root meaning that suggests incapacity and powerlessness. This dogma adds a protective enclosure to the Text by emphasizing its wondrousness and sanctifying its language.

At a time when creative energy had not yet abandoned the lands of Islam, this dogma served as a challenge, both explicit and implicit, to writers willing to test the boundaries of their art. It resulted in a healthy literary emulation that held nothing back, sure of its capacity to produce an equally stimulating and musical prose. I am thinking of the eleventh-century writer Abū 'l-Alā' al-Ma'arrī (died in 1058), the wise skeptic, blind and vegetarian, who lived in northern Syria, in Ma'rrat an-Nu'mān, a small town surrounded by groves of pistachio trees, a hundred miles south of Aleppo. Opinions in critical tradition posit that his *Risālat al-Ghufrān* was written with the intention of shattering the dogma of the inimitability of the Koran.[5] It is unsurprising that such a challenge should be met by this free-thinking poet and writer, a doubter and ironist whose tragic pessimism led him so far as to advocate the Buddhist practice of cremation so that, symbolically, believers honoring their dead would relinquish the myth-inspired hope in the resurrection of the body and the promise of eternal life in paradise.

This supposed undermining of *i'jāz* revived a polemic that had arisen in Baghdad among members of the *mu'tazila* school in the early ninth century, prior to the issuance of the dogma, with regard to the status to be granted Koranic discourse. The enlightened *mu'tazila* refuted the belief in an uncreated Koran—the belief that gave rise to the dogma in the first place—and posited a Koran produced in human time. In other words, without denying the divine origin of the text, they felt that the book circulating among the living is nothing but the materialization of the divine Word in human language. But this thesis was struck down by the political-theological authorities. Thus, the belief in an uncreated Koran shielded by its inimitability triumphed and became a commonplace in Islamic thought, supported by grammarians and rhetoricians who, in turn, took the argument several steps further to prove the splendor, richness and superhuman superiority of the literary and discursive performance of the Koranic text. Al-Ma'arrī's writings might well be a fierce reaction to the figments that already prevailed in the minds of his fellow Muslims, whether learned or unschooled.

4

The fiction that attributes the Koranic text to God produced another important effect on the collective imagination by contributing to the symbolic structuring of individual believers, who visualize through the Koran a concrete manifestation of the absolute located within their own physical boundaries, the same envelope of reality. It is thus in the very letter of the text (sustained vocally and graphically) that the Word is made incarnate, just as it is made flesh in the Christian tradition and embodied in the tablets of the Decalogue in Jewish representation. These powerfully distinct signifiers determine the change in creative energy from one to the other of the three monotheisms. Where, for Christians, the body is the signifier that advocates love of the image via painting and sculpture, the letter is the signifier in Islam that favors the calligrapher and cantor. The Jewish proscription of representation, on the other hand, remains consistent with the content of the second commandment of the tablet forbidding graven images, for the tablet was cracked when Moses threw it down in anger at the Israelites' worship of the Golden Calf, symbol of transgression and the Israelites' temporary regression to idolatry and the worship of images that prevailed at the time in Egypt, where they had only just been released from captivity by their prophet, who was both pontiff and prince.

With regard to the Koran, a fruitful tension came to exist between aesthetics and exegesis. The first magnified the letter as signifier and, in doing so, nourished the symbolic and imaginary side of the human psyche, particularly through psalmody and calligraphy. The exegete, on the other hand, sought to clarify meaning wherever anything equivocal, undeterminable, or strange occurred. Exegesis gave precedence to the signified, to meaning that, once determined, could be ascribed some practical function in real life. It is this tension that structured individuals by means of their relation to the Book. But once the fanatics of the signified triumph and seek to apply the letter to reality, there reigns a form of prescriptive reduction. It was ever thus. Today, those we call Islamists represent the zealots of the text reduced to its signified, canceling the aesthetics and metaphysics that sustain it, and restricting religious experience to the ostentatious practice of worship, which results in social censure and a kind of ideological indoctrination. In this situation, the act of calligraphy and the performance of the cantor lose the essence of their symbolic vocation as they gain in legibility and intelligibility; as this inverse proportion follows the curve of entropy in favor of an increasingly circumscribed signified, the focus will switch to imperatives that prescribe the licit and proscribe the illicit. The Holy Word then becomes a watchword intended to standardize the multitude of believers and lock them into a single mode of belief, an impoverished form of faith indeed. Even tastes bear witness to this mutilating mutation. Calligraphy has given way to the mechanized reproduction of easily recognizable standard lettering. As for psalmody, over the past two decades or so, the Wahhabi school has edged out the Egyptian school among Muslim listeners. Thus, we have moved away from a voice that veils the text in a strangeness all the more delightful for its excess, and toward an articulation of triumphant meaning, a reign of terror that divides all acts between reward and punishment.

5

I see no way to recover the symbolic function of the Koran other than reinvesting meaning with mystery or, to put it differently, returning the Text to its infinity, which would make interpretation a task without end, never complete, always begun anew, far from the naive truths and false facts that fanaticize the crowd. In the hands of the right interpreters, the Text will break with a current usage that has turned it into a moral, legal, and political handbook, one that has squandered the Book's aspiration to an absolute, an infinite. The Text needs to be stirred up not only by subjecting it to the interpreter's scrutiny but also by daring to tackle the issue of its origins and secure its place in history, as did Spinoza for the Bible in his *Tractatus Theologico-Politicus.*[6] Once this is accomplished, the next step would involve examining incongruities that occur throughout the traditional theological, exegetic, and spiritual corpus so as to return meaning to its undecided and equivocal basis, which springs not from hermeneutics alone but also from philological assessment derived from historically based criteria.

When it comes to exegesis, it is time to turn away from the manual of Ibn al-Kathīr (late thirteenth–early fourteenth centuries), currently in official use for its clarity, even oversimplification, of meaning, and which predisposes minds to receive the fundamentalist message.[7] In its place should be revived the densely rich inventory undertaken by Tabarī (ninth–tenth centuries), who brought together in his *Commentary* divergent viewpoints issuing from the first generations of believers, out of which he hoped to shape a tradition.[8] I would add the *Commentary* by Zamakhsharī (eleventh century) and *Keys to the Mystery* by Fakhr ad-Dīn Rāzī (twelfth century) for the density of their explanations, often weighed on the scales of reason.[9] These thinkers never hesitated to make use of the *Isrā'iliyāt*, that is, biblical and rabbinical writings, in order to flesh out or clarify certain Koranic notations that appeared furtive or terse. Indeed, the Koran implicitly invites this cross-referencing, for it evokes figures and stories in the form of biblical or quasi-biblical reminiscences that give heft to the Koranic text when the reader rediscovers them as they were expressed in an earlier form.

It is incumbent upon modernists and reformers to cultivate this region of traditional theology that has been left barren in the wake of Ibn al-Kathīr, all the way down to today's Islamists. The question of ties between the Koran, the Torah, and the Gospels should constitute at a symbolic level the dividing line between Muslim and Islamist. And to better establish the legitimacy of this textual exchange, we should be reminded that in the Islamic tradition, the People of Experience would read other revealed scriptures in their original versions. In thirteenth-century Damascus, the Sufi Ibn Hūd would hold seminars at his home where he would publicly comment on some passage or other from the Bible, and these sessions would be attended by Muslims as well as Jews.[10] Ibn ʿArabī recommended that anyone who professes Islam should also be familiar with the Bible. He even developed a reading protocol: accept everything put forward by the Bible that remains within the bounds of reason and does not contradict the Koran. The same Ibn ʿArabī often noted that the Scriptures are complementary when defining the states, the stations, and the abodes that the seeker encounters on the Path. For him, the Scriptures were revealed in the "Four Books" (Torah, Psalms, Gospels, Koran: *Tawrāt, Zābūr, Injīl, Qurʾān*).[11] And he remarks that it is no coincidence that the Bible and the Koran begin with the same letter, *b: baraʾa,* "to create," in the Bible, and *bism,* "in the name of," for the Koran.

It is also vital for the symbolic survival of the Koran as a signifying object to give serious consideration to the questions this book raises among researchers in order to gain maximum profit from the freedom and audaciousness, whether pertinent or not, that science can bring to the discussion. I am thinking of three areas of investigation in particular that have come together in recent years to reopen the field of inquiry regarding the Koran. It is here that the problematic symbolic function is being explored, the one so overlooked by Islamists, but which represents for Islam a productive reference that will structure the Muslim subject. I will cite first the epigraphist François Déroche and his attempt at reconstituting the first Koranic codex, thought to date from 660/670,[12] pieces of which are to be found among pages of writings from Medina now disseminated in several collections. The transcription *a minima* present on these pages (some would say the defective transcription) uses neither diacritical marks necessary for distinguishing consonants from one another, nor vowel markings that voice those consonants, providing a perfect illustration of the problems of opacity. This phonetic indeterminacy that characterizes the archival document legitimizes the philological work carried out by Christoph Luxenberg, who seeks to elucidate the obscurities of Koranic discourse by attempting to uncover the Syro-Aramaic beneath the Arabic.[13] This work has helped him reconstruct a discursive consistency missing in certain parts of the text, or at least such as it is read today by Muslims. Finally, the same lack of documents authorizes historian Alfred-Louis de Prémare to elaborate a story of how the Koran came to be written, by interpreting a number of details gleaned in chronicles from the first four centuries of the Hajīr with regard to the most vexing questions, as they were put forward in various controversies and polemics internal to Islam, and as they might be confronted by an outsider's viewpoint (essentially Christian) that was contemporary to the Muslim one.[14]

These attempts are worthwhile despite the tenuousness of their contribution, at times contested and easily refutable, especially when they systematize an approach with clear ideological aims (as is the case of Christoph Luxenberg, a pseudonym that conceals a Mesopotamian Christian concerned with gaining recognition for the historical glory of his community, articulated in Syriac and Neo-Aramaic). Nevertheless, what I feel makes these works so valuable is their willingness to take on the question of the Koran's historicity, a field I would like to see occupied by members of the Islamic faith as well. This would be the harbinger of an opening of the Muslim mind to the notion of freedom of inquiry, of critical thinking, a prerequisite on the path to truth at the risk of undermining the myths that undergird creed.

To summarize, any fresh Islamic approach to the Koran will be ineffective without the freedom to delve into the bolder aspects of Tradition (denied by today's Islam) and to take advantage of the work being carried out by modern Western research. These provisional truths will never get to the bottom of the Text's infinite meaning, of those seemingly useless areas that are so useful in generating myth, opening onto the vastness of the imagination and producing a malleable material for further symbolic elaboration.

From myth to history: this would seem to be the best direction for apprehending the Koran as a form that is always experienced in the present, always reformulated in the here and now. But this form should be experienced from within. When it comes to meaning, a fresh interpretation is imperative, one that takes into account the context of its first issuance but also liberates the Text from the constraints imposed by Tradition, whose most reductive and exclusive fundaments have been cultivated and radicalized by some groups. For our part, then, we need to return to that Tradition and seek out the discrepancies and gaps, the overflow of the text that will help us elaborate a meaning that is in step with our century. The next chapter addresses this exercise. The "clash of interpretations" that is considered in what follows constitutes one of the methods that will help us meet the challenge of civilization.

CHAPTER 2

## The Clash of Interpretations

In order to understand the emergence of Islamic fundamentalism and to devise the best means of resisting it, we need to go
back to the founding text, in all its ambivalence, and to engage
the conflict, if not the war, of interpretation. Fundamentalism
concerns first and foremost the way Islam relates to the two
earlier monotheisms, Judaism and Christianity. To investigate
more closely these other believers in the single Godhead, it is
important to consult the Koranic text itself and to scrutinize its
ambiguities. Two verses in particular could be considered emblematic of its ambivalence.

The first has come to be known in the exegetic tradition as
the War Verse (Koran 9:29) and is located in the *at-Tawba* sūra,
"The Repentance," the only one that does not begin with the
invocation of God the Merciful and Compassionate. This verse
says: "Fight those who do not believe in Allah or in the Last
Day, and who do not consider unlawful what Allah and His
Messenger have made unlawful, and who do not adopt the religion of truth from those who were given the Scripture. Fight
them until they give the *jizya* willingly while they are humbled."[1]

This is the verse invoked, for example, by the The Armed Islamic Group (GIA) terrorists who massacred the monks of Tibhirine in Algeria in 1996. The same verse is said to grant religious legitimacy to the suicide bombers of Hamas in Israel. The same reference may well have been involved in galvanizing the criminals responsible for the horrifying attacks on September 11, 2001, in New York and Washington, D.C. Thus, an ideological manipulation that resorts to holy scripture can provide legitimacy in a thousand-year-old exegetic tradition.

In effect, if we go back to various traditional commentaries, this verse would have us deny true belief in God to both Jews and Christians, and would coerce us to spread the notion of *true religion* by affirming that the one true religion is in fact Islam. As it happens, the Koran did not devise this notion, which actually goes back to Moses, as demonstrated by Jan Assmann in his book *Le Prix du monothéisme* (The Price of Monotheism).[2] The Koran merely updates and recycles the notion for its own sectarian ends. The idea begins to undermine its own purposes as soon as one realizes that this notion of true religion can be mirrored indefinitely, since a member of the faithful who adheres to an exclusive creed is by necessity always considered an infidel by those that he himself has deemed infidels. Herein begins the deconstruction of this concept[3] that even an acute mind like Pascal's cannot escape, for in his *Pensées*, with regard to his own belief, Christianity, or rather Catholicism, the subtle logician gets tangled up in this notion of true religion.

But getting back to the Koran, one has to realize that in the exegetic tradition, this verse is approached with a caution quite unlike the more radical use of it by fundamentalists today. The wording of the verse suggests what Jacques Berque calls "the conditional duty of war against the people of the Book."[4] It implicitly requires humble submission in exchange for protection, or conversion, or even death. In the course of conquest, this procedure was in force, even though a certain mythology in Islam would have it that a large proportion of the conquered populations were somehow predisposed to Islam. Historians also find a favorable argument in the fact that the states that had previously ruled over the various peoples that converted en masse to Islam had been unfair: Islam thus brought greater justice and equality to the indigenous populations of the vanquished territories.

It should be kept in mind that Islam won out over Christianity essentially in the part of the world that includes Palestine, Syria, Egypt, and the Maghreb. This observation raises a question that I believe worth consideration, for it represents a historical enigma: Why did local Christianity so thoroughly disappear from the Maghreb, while in Egypt and the Syro-Palestinian region it remains vital to this day, though an increasingly diminished minority, weakened but still present where it preexisted Islam? The end of Christianity in the Maghreb is often attributed to the zeal of the seventh- and eighth-century Berber dynasties (Almoravid and Almohad), strongly hegemonic and opposed to monotheistic minorities. Highly coercive when it came to their *dhimmis*, these dynasties most probably invoked this verse to carry out their assimilation operations.

This same verse continues to have devastating effects, with the more radical Muslim groups leaning on Koranic citations of this sort to combat what they call "Crusaders and sons of Zion," Christians and Jews, whom they reduce to "implacable enemies." The use of violence in the name of God is hardly a dead issue but is very much present in today's news, and all the more threatening in that it makes its claims in the name of Scripture. Moreover, fundamentalists are spreading the word that this bellicose verse belongs to the last revealed sūra. This warrior-like, irredentist dimension has thus superseded all others as the ultimate meaning of the divine message. As the radicals see it, this verse, which enjoys the advantage of having the last word, ends up abrogating some one hundred others that are more favorable to believers of the two other monotheisms, to whom they grant the dignity and distinction of being People of the Book.

And yet, as I see it, the Koran's true worth resides in the verses that these crazed literalists have canceled out, those that reveal another aspect of the Book, where recognition is granted to a profile resembling the man who stood on the Mount of Olives. Among the verses that trace a different path for Islam, I would distinguish the following: "Invite to the way of your Lord with wisdom and good instruction, and argue with them in a way that is best" (Koran 16:125). This latter expression (*bi'l-latī hiya aḥsan*) is frequently used in common discourse: Whenever a controversy or conflict arises, of whatever order, this expression is invoked to return the disagreement to a level of civility so as to avoid violence, even if the parties remain irreconcilable. This verse is referred to even in family matters, when dissent arises over a divorce, for instance, or an inheritance claim. Conciliatory voices resort to this expression to appease quarrels that tear us apart. "Invite to the way of your Lord with wisdom and good instruction, and argue with them in a way that is best. Indeed, your Lord is most knowing of who has strayed from His way, and He is most knowing of who is rightly guided." The same expression, "in a way that is best," is found elsewhere in the Holy Book: "And do not argue with the People of the Scripture except in a way that is best, except for those who commit injustice among them, and say, "We believe in that which has been revealed to us and revealed to you. And our God and your God is one; and we are Muslims in submission to Him" (Koran 29:46).

In the second part of verse 125 of sūra 16, "Indeed, your Lord is most knowing of who has strayed from His way, and He is most knowing of who is rightly guided," exegetes agree to identify the "rightly guided" with Islam, and indeed are probably often biased in their commentary. But objectively, the letter of the text leaves undetermined the identity of these "rightly guided." Nothing in the verse requires that only Islam be acknowledged.

In April 2003, I went to Iran, more precisely to Isfahan, to participate in a gathering organized by the Foundation for

Dialogue among Civilizations, where participants included professors from the world over, notably from important American universities. Among them was even one of the signatories to the letter on "just war,"[5] a manifesto drawn up by some sixty American intellectuals and academics to support the war in Afghanistan in response to the September 11, 2001, aggression (their statement was based notably on Saint Augustine and his *City of God*, in which he justifies war against barbarity in the name of civilization). Representing the most nationalist viewpoint possible, these American professors expressed themselves in good faith. There were impassioned discussions, with many diverse opinions, in a frank, academic confrontation of ideas and a spirit of lively debate in accordance with the codes of civility that govern academic disputation. This took place during a time of openness in Iran, when the country was led by the moderate liberal Khatami.[6] The host foundation, which was a private institution, represented the approach of liberal partisans of the president in office.

The gathering was opened by a man of religion, an official of the Islamic state, wearing the mullah's robe and turban. He began by urging all guests to express themselves sincerely. The American academics had been invited to develop their ideas in all frankness, since, if discussion was to take place, the hosts had to understand their positions clearly. The meeting had begun with some chanting of the Koran. The cantor sat behind his lectern, the Koran open before him, and the meeting was placed under the auspices of the verse that I have just quoted, moderated by an expert voice: "Invite to the way of your Lord with wisdom and good instruction, and argue with them in a way that is best. Indeed, your Lord is most knowing of who has strayed from His way, and He is most knowing of who is rightly guided." In these circumstances, the end of the verse shone forth objectively, in an absolute and transhistoric manner, removing from circulation the notion of true religion, temporarily suspending it, deferring it, leaving to divine enigma the distinction between true and false, right and wrong, the

straight and crooked paths. In the end, the distinction vanished, withdrawing into divine mystery. At the very instant this
verse resounded, it was definitively removed from traditional
identification, which justifies its position once it considers Islam as the one true way. According to the text's own logic, both
discursive and grammatical, we can legitimately move forward
with this loose interpretation that frees up meaning, leaving it
undetermined and open to discussion.

The other element to remember with regard to the second
positive verse that I quoted, where the same expression, "in a
way that is best," appears, is the way it invokes a code of civility
for discussing differences, divergence of opinion. Let me emphasize the appeal made in this verse, because some would
transcribe the word *Allah* as if it meant a God apart. On the
contrary, this verse explicitly rejects this interpretation. "We
believe in that which has been revealed to us and revealed to
you." This sentence thus puts into perspective the truth carried
forward by previous Scripture. "Our God and your God is
one."[7]

Out of this conviction emerged the judicial status of the
*dhimmi*, which at the time was a liberal, progressive move, for
it granted a place to the believers of another faith living in a
city ruled over by an Islamic authority. This notion was later
adapted and written into canon law by Alfonso X when he
came to power in Seville, thereby allowing for the coexistence
of monotheisms in the wake of his reconquest in the mid–
thirteenth century. This Catholic prince was to rule over Muslim subjects, to whom he granted the same *dhimmi* status that
they had applied to their Christian and Jewish subjects when
they were the rulers of Al-Andalus.

The illuminations that illustrate the *Cantigas de Santa Maria*
testify to the presence of Jewish and Muslim minorities in the
city under the Catholic prince's rule. We see them busy at work
at a number of productive crafts, participating in the enrichment and embellishment of the city. We also discover them in
leading roles alongside their Christian counterparts, associated

with such noble activities as chess, courtly music, or the imparting of theoretical knowledge or practical technical or artistic skill.[8] In doing so, they were internaling the spirit of chivalry, while also perpetuating the *futūwa* of their Arab genealogy, the code of honor assimilated by the guildsmen of the various crafts.[9] The atmosphere of mutual understanding emanating from these images is in fact an extension of the climate created by the *dhimmi* status applied at the time when a Muslim prince reigned over these Andalusian cities.

The reversal of the roles of dominant and dominated seemed to result in a viable status that the Muslims could henceforth accommodate, now that they had become subjects of the Christian monarch. We see evidence of this in the meaning suggested by the Arabic inscriptions that join in the decor of the Alcazar in Seville, final avatar of the architectural style known as Hispano-Moorish in the second half of the fourteenth century, whose model remains the Alhambra of Granada. Indeed, the craftsmen who built the Alcazar were Muslims who belonged to a guild in Toledo (as noted in an inscription), and the calligraphers do not hesitate to use the same formulas once dedicated to the Muslim prince to acknowledge the Christian sponsor, Pedro the First, or the Cruel. Thus, one reads scrolled all along the upper section of the walls: "Glory to Sultan Don Pedro" (*al-'izzū li's-Sultān Dūn Bidrūor*).

In the same period, and under the same reign, another monument, this time Jewish, confirms the viable adoption by Catholics of the notion of *dhimmi*. In Toledo, in the synagogue of Transito, one can still see today the coexistence of Hebrew and Arabic text via a monumental calligraphy deployed in geometric and floral figures, carved and sculpted into plaster according to the Hispano-Moorish style used to embellish the princely dwellings of Seville. Thus, classical Arabic eulogies abide alongside biblical citations, notably from the Psalms, Chronicles, and the Book of Habakkuk. One segment of the inscriptions reveals that the synagogue was dated and signed by master mason Don Meir Abdeil in 1357, who built it at the request of

Samuel Ben Meir Ha-levi Abū'l-Afia, treasurer of Pedro the Cruel, whose glories were praised using the same Arabic formula that festooned the Alcazar in Seville.[10]

This relative acknowledgment of the other was to disappear from Catholic Spain at the end of the fifteenth century, with the onset of the militant, fanatical Inquisition. It was to resurface, however, among the authors of the Enlightenment, who saw it as an early form of progress, and who would go on to radically transform the law by freeing it from its theologically based reference. We find it mentioned in Locke's *Letter Concerning Tolerance* (1689) and Voltaire's *Treatise on Toleration* (1763), as well as the entry for "Tolerance" in Voltaire's *Dictionnaire philosophique* (1764). Both these authors pointed to the relative progress of Islam concerning the problem of intolerance that Europe was experiencing during the same period, France in particular, where Catholic violence during the wars of religion had resulted in massacres. Let us recall that the philosopher Ferney reacted with his *Treatise* to the Calas affair in Toulouse, the last gasp of fanaticism by the religious majority against the reformed minority. The English philosopher and French writer alike expressed a tempered admiration for the way the Grand Turk managed religious pluralism in the city where the Ottoman Porte cast a long shadow: Muslims attempting to convert were punished with the full force of the law, but at the same time the state acknowledged a legitimate place for non-Muslim believers in Scripture that predated the coming of Islam.

The privilege granted to the *dhimmi*, the non-Muslim, is mentioned by yet another witness: Lady Montagu, wife of the English ambassador to the Ottoman Porte.[11] In her now widely known body of letters, the English lady notes among the Ottoman elite a remarkable mentality, admiring their religious openness.[12] This elite was influenced by what is called Akbarism, that is, the theory of the great mystic and philosopher Ibn 'Arabī, born in Murcia, Spain, in 1165 and dying in Damascus in 1240, who was honored by his disciples under the name Shaykh al-Akbar, or "Greatest Master." In the spiritual tradition of Sufism, of which Ibn 'Arabī is one of the most eloquent representatives, the two aforementioned Koranic verses constitute the reference that authorizes the seeker to go to whatever lengths are necessary to acknowledge the other's religion.

These two verses of relative acknowledgment were to open a breach into which the seekers on the Sufi path would find the latitude to broaden their scope of experience. In theological tradition, we observe a doctrinal accord between Islam and Judaism with regard to the suspicion of idolatry in Christianity, an accord that would result in the categorical rejection of the notion of the Trinity. This was a regularly disputed point in various controversies involving the doctors of Islam and Christianity. John of Damascus, a Father of the Church, who was for a time in the service of the Ummayad Muslim state, provides an early testimony of this, dating back to the eighth century. In one of his texts against Islam, this pillar of the Church gave a stinging response: "If we are, as you say, Associators,[13] then I, in turn, will accuse you of being mutilators." It could indeed be said that Muslims are "mutilators" since they have amputated important features of Christian belief in their version.While Muslims make mention of certain episodes such as the Annunciation, the Nativity, and the Presentation at the Temple, they leave out the Crucifixion, the Resurrection, and the Redemption, and shatter the fundamentals of the Trinity and the divine persons. The Father of the Church argues point by point: to the charge of "association" by Muslims, to be taken as meaning idolatry, he replies with a charge of "mutilation" against the Muslim, considered a heretic. The Greek term used by John is effective here: *koptàs*, which literally means slicing into live flesh, or finely chopping.[14] The Trinity, divine persons, the mysteries of hypostasis, all such issues are utterly unthinkable in Islam.

And yet, here is Ibn 'Arabī lifting the taboo in a poem where, as a Muslim, he sings the praises of the Trinity:

1. At Dhu Salam and the monastery in the abode of al-Hima, are gazelles Who show thee the sun in the forms of marble statues.

2. Therefore I watch spheres and serve in a church and guard a many-Colored meadow in the spring.

3. And at one time I am called the herdsman of the gazelles in the desert, And at another time I am called a Christian monk and an astrologer.

4. My Beloved is three although He is One, even as the (three) Persons (of the Trinity) are made one Person in essence.

5. So be not displeased, O friend, that I speak of gazelles that move Round the marble statues as "a shining sun,"

6. Or that I use metaphorically the necks of the gazelles, the face of the Sun, and the breast and wrist of the white statue,

7. Just as I have lent to the branches (spiritual) endowments and to the Meadows more qualities, and to the lightning laughing lips.[15]

This piece is composed according to a poetics of the obscure, defying explanation, a quality that has been conserved in the translation. The middle line of this poem, the fourth line, states the dogma of the Trinity. In his own commentary—Ibn 'Arabī comments on all his poems—the poet tells us that, where in traditional Arabic-language prosody each line must offer a single meaning, he has innovated by bestowing three meanings on each, in honor of the principle of three in the very structure of the poem. You notice that gazelles, suns, and statues appear in the first line. In the second, "I watch spheres" points to the act engendered by a relation to the sun; "I serve in a church" refers to the evocation of the statues, which honors Christian iconophilia; "I am a herdsman" marks the third act, brought about by gazelles. In his commentary, the poet says that one of the peculiarities of the Christian scene is the love of images, illustrated by the presence of statues in their temples. This characteristic marks a radical difference with the Muslim place of worship which, like the Jewish synagogue, is devoid of iconography of any sort. Thus, the second line stages three acts: "I watch spheres / I serve in a church / I guard a many-colored meadow in the spring," and three meanings dwell in correspondence with the three precepts that animate the first.

In the third line, we move from act to name, from gesture to the function or role of the actor: "And at one time I am called the herdsman of the gazelles in the desert, / And at another time I am called a Christian monk and an astrologer." One follows the linkage in all three lines between "gazelles," "meadow/ guard," and "herdsman"; between "sun," "sphere," and "astrologer"; between "statues," "church," and "monk." "Herdsman," "monk," and "astrologer" parse out the three meanings borne by the three names of the third line. We then read the fourth line, reserved for Christian dogma. It is followed by three others, each of which in turn deploys three meanings. The fifth stages a scene resembling a rite associated with the three initial figures: the gazelles wandering about the statues lit by the sun. And the sixth enriches each of our three figures with an extra meaning (the faces that give the sun its powers of multiplying and transforming;[16] the shape of the gazelle's neck, symbol of the muezzin's vocalization of the call to prayer; the breast and wrist, which bestow spiritual power on the statues). The seventh line ends the poem by again combining the three meanings, associating two terms each time, to illustrate the two levels of trope at which the poem as a whole is functioning (branches/endowments, meadows/qualities, lightning/lips).

Thus is honored the ternary principle, not only in its doctrine but within the form that adorns the poem, in its structure, its scansion, by virtue of each line channeling three meanings. Furthermore, the poem is a vertical manifestation of the Three, since it is made up of seven lines. The central line speaks of the Trinity, expressing the mystery of the divine persons. It is preceded by three lines and followed by three more. Thus, the number of lines is seven, which is the third odd number (after three and five). The number one does not count as an odd number, for it is the matrix that opens the chain of numbers into infinity. Hence, the articulation between the horizontal uneven number set (illustrated by the first odd number) and the vertical set (based on the third odd number) confirms and reinforces the figure Three, the fundament of the Trinity.

The poem is thus the concrete embodiment of affinity between image, chant, and word, unified by rhythm, just as Ezra Pound conceived of it.[17] In his view, the most active intensity of meaning is produced by a three-part process. The first, which Pound called *phanopoeia*, consists of projecting a visual image into the mind. Our poem, with its sun, statues, and gazelles, is highly visual. Next come the emotional correlations through the sound and rhythm of speech, or *melopoeia*, also assumed throughout by Ibn 'Arabī, with his ternary scansion. Finally, through a process Pound called *logopoeia*, a poem stimulates intellectual or emotional associations already present in the receiver's conscious mind among actual words or word groups employed. Our poem deploys three chains of association, each of which gets doubled: (1) among gazelles, herder, desert, meadow, branches; (2) among sun, sphere, astrologer, lightning, face, laughing lips; (3) among statue, wrist, bust, church, monk, qualities.

We thus are compelled to conclude that oddness, or imparity, is as basic to the poem as to the analysis thereof. Both the ternary and the first odd number are present in the explanation of the poem built on the uneven number, since poems in general are determined as tripartite (image, melody, idea). These three axes clarify and enlighten the poem devoted to the Trinity via systematic recourse to this feature, and in all fields of the ternary. Thus, there is an absolute consistency between the means of realizing the poem and the instruments used to interpret it. This feedback loop of imparity is present, and delightfully so, even in the echo resonating between the poem and its gloss, which extends and expands its impact. Here, the interpretation is an integral part of the poem's economy and provides its ultimate accomplishment.

Furthermore, imagining himself faced by an interlocutor, in the fifth line, Ibn 'Arabī writes: "So be not displeased, O friend," for he is fully aware that he is addressing his fellow Muslims in their own language. And he knows that such discourse will strike his readers as unprecedented, which is why he resorts to the rhetoric of persuasion: he produces speech acts, as Austin has defined them, meant to convince a readership unused to hearing such affirmations.

In his commentary, Ibn 'Arabī goes so far as to consider that the "three in one" doctrine is honored within the Koran by the plurality of God's names—ninety-nine in all, called *asmā' Allah al-husnā*, or the best names of God. Ibn 'Arabī ascribes special meaning, in his general theory, to this scriptural numbering, and adds that it is no coincidence that, out of the ninety-nine names, three stand out in the Koran: Ar-Rab, or the Lord, Ar-Rahman, or the Merciful, and Allah, or simply God. The fact that there are three names thus sanctioned by the Word is, according to Ibn 'Arabī, an implied reference to the Trinity, whose followers, he explicitly states, pray in the name of "the Father, the Son and the Holy Spirit, in one God." This is how the switch of pronoun in line four becomes intelligible. The shift from one hemistich to the other of the personal pronoun from the first person singular to the third person plural means the following: I, a Muslim, love the One God that becomes Three (according to the Koranic theory of Names, and with reference to my Holy Book's electing to emphasize Allah, ar-Rabb, and ar-Rahmān), as do the Christians who, in their faith, believe in the Trinity and in hypostases (which are designated by an Arabic form of an old Syriac Neo-Aramaic term, *uqnum*, or the plural *aqānīm*).

This poem provides a sign of that willingness to roam the outer reaches by visiting the other's symbolic domain. Ibn 'Arabī knew that, in these wanderings, he could be as bold as he wished, even if it meant offending Muslims and often arousing their fury. For such statements are considered blasphemous, punishable by death according to the Law. Had the religious legal authorities taken action against the daring statements of the Sufi master, they would clearly have been mistaken. For Ibn 'Arabī is secure in the knowledge that everything he proposes springs directly from his reading of the sacred text, from his understanding of revelation. What some called scandalous was nothing but interpretation of meanings laid down in the Koran itself. But such meanings remain concealed to most. This is why, in another poem, Ibn 'Arabī wonders how opportune it is to make public certain of his Koranic interpretations, since, at the time, they were so likely to be associated with the worst sin of all, idolatry:

> Oftentimes do I extract the substance of a doctrine.
> Were I to divulge it, they would say to me:
> "You are among the worshipers of idols!"
> Men of Islam would call for my death:
> Believing themselves righteous, they would be in grave error.[18]

It is in this light, and at the risk of this hermeneutic acuity, that Ibn 'Arabī elaborates his rigorous theory of sainthood.[19] It centers on the notion that the legacy of prophets prior to Islam ought to be assumed within Islam itself. He recommends that the faithful, within their own belief system, live by the partial truths handed down by the various prophets that traverse pre-Islamic history, ones that the Koran alludes to either implicitly or explicitly. They are figures destined to reappear within the far vaster horizon opened by the Koran. In this economy of sainthood, we saw how Ibn 'Arabī oversteps the bounds of the Koran to recommend the reading of other books, that is, the Torah, the Psalms, and the Gospels. Again, this protocol can be summed up in two principles: not to accept anything that clashes with reason, anything extraordinary that breaks with the real world, including the realm of the miraculous; and not to believe in the books of others when these clearly contradict one's own Scriptures.

How else does Ibn 'Arabī demonstrate his tolerance of the other? In order to respect the law of hospitality and to provide a munificent welcome to his monotheistic counterparts, he undertakes etymologies that I would call more spiritual than philological. For instance, he bases the word *yahūdi*, meaning Jewish, on the nominal form *huda*, a major Koranic term signifying "the straight path," making Jews "those who walk in righteousness." Hence, by means of a spiritual etymology, he ascribes to the Jews an ethical primacy as they themselves have appropriated it, as they experience it within themselves. For the word *naçāra*, which designates Christians, Ibn ʿArabī goes beyond accepted etymology that traces the word to Jesus of Nazareth, to associate the birthplace of Christ, Nāçira in Arabic, with the noun *nuçra*, which means "help to one's neighbor" or "love of one's neighbor." Here again, Ibn ʿArabī takes into account the specific ethical orientation that Christians claim as their own.

Since I have dwelled quite a bit on Ibn ʿArabī, I would like to recount an anecdote that he tells, which is appropriate to my point. When he was once in Mecca, he met a man from Cordova (Mūsa ibn Muhammad) who told him the story of a man from Qairawān that he had met in the holy city. This pious Qairawāni recounted the series of circumstances that had led him to make the pilgrimage. He was surely what is called in the spiritual tradition a "master of scruple." One evening, he made up his mind to undertake the pilgrimage to Mecca. He then wondered, "How will I travel? By land or by sea?" This became a quandary with no easy solution. To put his mind at ease, he declared, "I shall ask the first person I come upon at dawn." Upon leaving his home the next morning, he happened upon a Jew. At first, he was disconcerted but, emboldened, he asked him, "O Jew, I solicit your advice on a matter concerning my journey: Should I travel by land or by sea?" And the Jew replied, "By God! Someone of your stature should ask such a question? Do you not see that in your own Book, God says to you, 'It is He who enables you to travel on land and sea' (Koran 10:22)? He puts land ahead of sea. Is there not herein a secret of God? What is best for you is what He placed first; and He placed the sea in last place that the voyager use it as a last resort." The pilgrim was pleasantly surprised by these words and set out on his journey taking the land route. "And by God,

never did I have such a journey, so blessed by the divine, beyond anything I could have hoped."[20]

Thus, in medieval times, it was not unheard of for a Jew to
be familiar enough with Muslim scripture to recite an appropriate passage for the circumstance. He possessed not only
textual knowledge but also interpretative skill that shed light
on a text's meaning. The Jew had memorized the Muslim
Book, claimed authority to gloss it, and, in doing so, acknowledged its holiness while at the same time coming up with a
piece of advice that his interlocutor graciously accepted. Not
only that, the Jew's advice was experienced by the Muslim who
followed it as corroborated by divine order, to the point that
God showered blessings upon the traveler who took the advice
to heart. Is it any coincidence that the man from Cordova who
recounted this anecdote of Judeo-Muslim complicity to Ibn
'Arabī should bear the names of the two prophets of revelation,
Mūsa for the Jews and Muhammad for the Muslims?

This anecdote has all the hallmarks of an apologue, or even a
study in anthroponomastics. It provides a perfect illustration of
the sort of substitution that enriches the dynamics of hospitality.
The host is substituted by the guest, the foreigner, who temporarily adopts the workings of the other's belief system to enlighten
him as to what had remained heretofore obscure, providing the
right answer based on the host's own frame of reference. This
substitution of Jew for Muslim does not ask much, in fact, of
the person performing it. Technically, it demonstrates the similarities of the two hermeneutics, the Koranic and the Midrashic
exegetic traditions. The art of interpretation proceeds in much
the same manner. The Koranic *ta'wīl* performed by the Jew can
be read as the substitute for a Talmudic mechanism. His *re-
sponsa* of a Jewish kind stands in for an Islamic *fatwa*.

By extension, is it not possible to obtain from this story the
Jewish equivalent of the Akbarism that pervades the oeuvre of
Ibn 'Arabī? This is a staging of the same structure that circu-
lates from one belief system to another: The theatricality of

substitution is played out in the heart of the Islamic city, animated by the cohabitation and conviviality that *dhimmi* status ensures, a status that will be made obsolete, of course, once democracy introduces the notion of citizen equality.

This is my personal view of the situation of Islam, and the examples just given are far from rare, only two or three among a dense body of texts. It is a state of mind that has existed in Islam, and was once interiorized by the political elite, as testifies Lady Montagu in her encounter with people in the service of the Ottoman state in the eighteenth century.

Within Islam, therefore, we see the literary premise, the discursive conditions, the scriptural elements capable of fueling the modern turn. But the tragedy of today's Islam is its resistance to this turn toward modernity, its stubborn refusal to borrow, its hostility to transfers from elsewhere. It has also created a situation where it has declared a war without the means of waging it, since the driving force of war is power, and today's Islam is dispossessed of its power. At very most, those who commit acts of violence today in the name of Islam are capable of doing damage, but their activism is doomed to fail historically, again due to their powerlessness. In fundamentalist and terrorist activism, the backward part of the Koran wins over the other part, the one that promises a future where the duty of respect for difference would have a place in our cities.

Another sūra that illustrates ambivalence is sūra 5, *al-Maʾida*, or "The Table Spread," which pushes the Koran's apparent contradictions as far as they will go. Traditional exegesis has had a hard time grappling with this sūra, and Western readers despair of understanding the polar opposites that it seems to convey, for it would appear to move from denunciation to salvation of Jews and Christians. It also contains a number of verses that spell out food prohibitions, which are in turn contradicted in a later verse that locates God's judgment not in compliance with taboos, but in the ethical quest.[21] I limit myself to two verses to illustrate this spirit of contradiction.

Let us begin with the one that seems to attack Jews and
Christians: "O you who have believed, do not take the Jews and
Christians as allies [*awliyā*]" (Koran 5:51). Read only for itself,
this verse is a favorite of fundamentalists, who cast the other
monotheists as the enemy, to be avoided or even struck down.
But placed within the context of the whole sūra, the verse gets
diluted by this other one: "Indeed, those who have believed
in the Prophet Muhammad and those before him who were
Jews or Sabians or Christians—those among them who believed in Allah and the Last Day and did righteousness [*'amala
çālihān*]—no fear will there be concerning them, nor will they
grieve" (5:69). Thus, after recommending the separation from
Jews and Christians, the Koran promises in the same sūra salvation for all, even for deists and agnostics. Apokatastasis here
finds its Koranic basis. Further, it is here that the ethical vocation becomes the criterion for salvation, beyond any consideration of belief in any so-called true religion.

This ethical calling becomes clear as both Law and Creed
are superseded: in both cases, the primacy of ethics crystallizes
in the same expression, repeated according to the variant that
introduces the passage from singular to plural, from one of the
verses cited above to the next, the first in a footnote (*'amilū aç-
çalihāt*, 5:93) and the second in the body of the text (*'amala
çālihān*, 5:69).

Two remarks are in order concerning verse 69 of this sūra.
First, in the Arabic, the Jews are designated not in a nominal
but in a verbal form, a neologism that says something to the
effect that they practice Judaism, that they "Judaïze" (*hādū*), as
if the Koranic text wished to emphasize the active ritual aspects of their worship, with its rules and rites that govern all
parts of daily life. In short, the Koran acknowledges that, to be
a Jew, one must do all things Jewishly, "Judaïze." And the verb
*hādū* seems to corroborate the Akbarian etymology that, as I
stated earlier, extracts the word "Jew" or *yahūdī* from *hudā*, the
"straight path," all these terms based on the same three-letter
root, *h d ā*, whose third form pattern can accommodate the

Koranic verb *hādū*, with the meaning of "doing things Jew-ishly," where in common speech it means "to give someone a gift." It is as if, through this play of homonyms, the Koranic text is suggesting that the Jews brought humanity the gift of ethics.

Next, in this same verse, reference is made to the Sabeans (*aç-çābi'ūn*) prior to any mention of Christians (*an-naçārā*). This enigmatic term refers to the third category of believers in-cluded in the People of the Book. Exegetic tradition identifies them sometimes as Zoroastrians, other times as Neoplatonists, surviving in the Harrān region of northern Mesopotamia until the tenth century, and still other times as Buddhists, a way for the Muslims of Iraq, Iran, and central Asia or India to extend to their neighbors of other faiths the possibility of partial acknow-ledgment, thereby making contact more legitimate and peaceful. Maimonides also adopts the notion, and sees in these Mesopo-tamian idolaters and astrologers the cradle of Abraham, whose intuition led him to the One God, creator of the objects they worshipped (the stars, the sun, the moon),[22] an intermediary stage that will lead to Moses, the first to associate prophecy with the receiving of a message revealed by listening to divine word.[23]

For the overall succinctness of sūra 5, I recommend Michel Cuypers's masterful analysis:[24] The apparent contradictions scattered throughout the text get resolved by establishing a hi-erarchy of meaning based on the rhetorical intensity of the various verses. By applying to this sūra of 120 verses the Se-mitic rhetorical grid devised by Bible scholars, Cuypers comes to distinguish the contextual from the perpetual, the ephem-eral from the permanent. Thus, what is at issue in this sūra is a *theology of religions* stating the impossibility of fulfilling the dream of abolishing a previous religion with the arrival of a newer one. No, Christianity will not make Judaism obsolete. Nor will Islam exhaust Judaism and Christianity. The destiny of the three monotheisms is to thrive simultaneously in their difference, with their resemblances coexisting with their dis-tinctiveness. It cannot be otherwise, as each of the three expresses the staging of the same sacrifice according to a different modality. What will matter most is the ethical emulation within a diversity of approaches,[25] as in the plurality of laws, the forms of worship and ritual. One verse is particularly revealing in this regard: "To each of you We prescribed a law and a method. Had Allah willed, He would have made you one nation, united in religion, but He intended to test you in what he has given you; so race to all that is good [*istabiqū al-khayrāt ilā Allah*]" (Koran 5:48).

Notice that in order to express ethical rivalry, the Koran uses a metaphor evoking an athletic competition. This same reference to athletics can be found in an article by Claude Levi-Strauss that might provide a key to understanding this seemingly contradictory, or at least paradoxical, sūra. It appeared in 1949, during the author's American period, when the world had just emerged from global war and was on the verge of the polarizing effects of the Cold War. This article deals with the foreign policy of a society still considered "primitive" at that time, an Amazonian society called the Nambikwara, with whom the author spent several months in 1938.[26] Written in a historical context between war and peace, it contains both implicit and explicit lessons for the present day. The point he makes is that violence against one group by another opens up the possibility of partnership. But Levi-Strauss concludes his piece by stating that we have lost that potential; we no longer think of humanity "as an ensemble of concrete groups among whom a constant balance must be established between competition and aggression, with mechanisms prepared in advance to soften the extremes liable to emerge in both camps. We have managed to conserve this institutional scheme only in the area of competitive athletics, that is, in the form of games, while in most primitive societies, we find it put into practice to resolve the most important problems of social life."[27] In the verse just cited, the Koran makes use of the sport metaphor to seek a balance between competition and aggression. It is as if it had anticipated the sports exception in human relations, and made of it the quintessential metaphor of ethical emulation designed to lean more toward competition compared to aggression, which is neither repressed nor discounted, but taken into account, all the better to reduce and contain it. Whatever the case, we ought to ponder this peculiar situation whereby what is considered exceptional in our times is found at the heart of a Koranic text, unless one considers that the Koran itself is a text issuing from the same cultural level as the one still known in 1949 as a "primitive society." If such is the case, then just as Levi-Strauss hoped to draw lessons for our time from the policies of the Nambikwara, we might be able to learn something from the Koran so that in our present time, each group will think of itself "in relation to, and in opposition to other groups," in order to constitute "a balancing factor between the ideal of total peace that amounts to utopia, and an equally total war which results from the unilateral system in which our civilization is blindly engaged."[28]

This sūra goes right to the heart of the Koran, the last of the three revealed Books. Does not the third verse affirm, "This day I have perfected for you your religion"? This assertion points decisively to a closure, wresting from the hands of fundamentalists the warlike meaning, which they consider as final and conclusive, as they see sūra 9 as the last revealed in the Koran, as I pointed out earlier in this chapter. I conclude that the conflict, if not clash or war, of interpretations must necessarily be declared once again. They are still ahead of us, and the fate of Islam (and of the world) hangs in the balance. We must fight on this front, with common sense, with a display of hospitality and a break with hostility.

Koranic verses that appear to stir up hostility need to be neutralized, situated in a context that goes beyond the moment of their appearance. They were decreed so that the new alliance would win followers and vie for a place in a religious scene already heavily occupied. These verses, like those of war or the saber (which have not been evoked here),[29] belong to the part of the Koran that is outmoded, perishable, a thing of the past, while those that teach philoxenia, the acknowledgment of otherness, along with those based on the laws of hospitality as tested by ethical emulation, are abundantly present in the lasting part of the Koran, urging us to be vigilant and to act in favor of a policy of everlasting peace that today more than ever should top our agenda, without suppressing altogether the share of aggression that inevitably comes along with the collaboration of self and other.

This distinction between temporary and eternal in the Koranic text was already made in the 1970s and '80s by the innovative Sudanese thinker Muhammad Mahmūd Tahā in his essay *The Second Message of Islam*.[30] In this book, the author features the early revelations in particular, those of Mecca where the entire human race is being addressed ("O Ye People," *Yā ayyuhā 'n-Nās*): The message is thus ascribed a universal dimension, ensuring its longevity. This part constitutes what Tahā calls the "second message of Islam," which is yet to come. Its rank as earliest means that later revelations take on secondary importance, those announced in Medina, for instance, where only the believers in the new creed are addressed ("O Believers," *Yā ayyāhā 'l-Ladhīna āmanū*), which reduces the transmission of meaning to a *particular* community that is subjected to the politics and laws of a specific place and time, circumstances that will inevitably change. These politico-judicial provisions, including slavery, polygamy, *jihād*, and *hudūd* (penal sanctions that translate into corporal punishment), as well as more general forms of inequality between the sexes or among believers, *dhimmis*, and pagans—all of these make up the obsolete side of the religion that, when practiced in modern times, represents an impediment to the evolution of law, manners, and individual consciousness.

These latter aspects belong to what Tahā calls "the first message of Islam," which has already produced its effect and now is part of the past. The proper term for this Islam is *imān*—belief—as the particular religion shaped during the latter Medina period. The Islam of *imān* appeared and was transcended at identifiable moments in history. *Islām*, on the other hand, is the religion that both predates and postdates that historical moment, a more "natural" *islām* that has existed somehow outside *imān*. Does the Koran not say that Abraham was a follower of the *islām* prior to the Islam-*imān*?[31] And this older Islam, witness to the first religious feeling, is also thriving within other beliefs that endure after the advent of Islam-*imān*: one might even find traces in Pascal's *Pensées* that suggest the notion of submission (the initial meaning of the word *islām*), one of the fundaments of Christianity perceived as the "one true faith."[32] The idea of submission also brings to a close fragment 233, devoted to the wager: "If this discourse pleases you and seems impressive, know that it is made by a man who has knelt, both before and after it, in prayer to that Being, infinite and without parts, *before whom he lays* all he has, for you also to *lay before him* all you have for your own good and for his glory, so that strength may be given to lowliness."[33] Thus do we acknowledge in this Christian writer the posture of *islām* referring to the sole, universal religion that dwells within each particular religion.

According to Tahā, this second Islam has remained historically suspended, in reserve, as a deferred coming, an advent always in the future, always coming, never arriving. It is addressed to all mankind, who see it as a promise. This openness motivates the sūrāt received in Mecca, the ones bearing witness to the universal religion in reserve behind all individual religions.[34]

Such an interpretive proposition upends the technique of abrogation (*naskh*), which belongs to the science of *tafsīr*, or traditional Koranic commentary. According to this practice, in case of flagrant contradiction, the later verse abrogates the earlier verse. Fundamentalists use and abuse this principle, for they dream of ascribing the rank of final revelation to sūra 9, so that verses 5 and 29, those of the saber and war, will have the last word and favor hostility, thereby abrogating, need I reiterate, more than one hundred verses whose meaning is favorable to Jews and Christians. Tahā's reading results in an

inversion of this chronological operation by granting the power
of abrogation to what was revealed earliest, in Mecca, and to
anything in the Medina revelations that retains a Meccan influence. For these two colorations, the Mecca and Medina
aspects of the Koran, can very well coexist within the same
sūra, as is the case with sūra 5. Thus, Tahā's reading indirectly
corroborates the hierarchy of meaning that strikes a balance
between competition and aggression that results in the meticu-
lous rhetorical technique applied by Michel Cuypers.[35] Two
ways of seeing come together, one theological and political, the
other discursive, so that the Koranic message that comes across
most strongly is the one that stresses ethical duty over obedience to Law, over hostility toward religious difference, notably the monotheistic religions. But this privilege conferred
upon ethical emulation is not put forward as an evasion but
as a way of arriving at an equilibrium between competition
and aggression, to use Levi-Strauss's terms, in the imposition of
a hierarchy of meaning that favors ethical duty, and meant to
lessen violence toward other competing faith communities.

It is this significance, in the end, that should be gleaned
from sūra 5, the last one to be revealed in Medina after the return of the Prophet to Mecca (to accomplish the Farewell Pilgrimage right before his death). This sūra is imbued with the
Mecca spirit as much as the Medina spirit. How does it resolve
the inherent contradiction of its message? By establishing a hierarchy of meaning to dispel all ambiguity and to assign first
place to the acknowledgment of diversity, according to a metaphysical policy based on coexistence and hospitality. It is always
important to seek out the hints of universal religion tucked into
the folds of any particular religion, in order to favor ethical
emulation and to temper violence against foreigners to a belief
system.[36]

As we draw nearer to this universal religion, it is possible to
adapt to the precondition that will remove us from the religious sphere altogether and ground us in poetry. The plan

would be to move from the Koran to the Diwan, that is, to follow the path, but in the opposite direction from the one advocated by the Holy Book,[37] which disqualifies poets, for Scripture was surely in keen competition with poetry, which was capable of staking out this alternative path.

# CHAPTER 3

# On the Arab Decline

To be Arab today is first of all a source of pride, to descend from an immense intellectual and creative tradition. But it also denotes a sadness linked to a feeling of decline, uneasiness, and monumental failure. One cannot but be struck by the gap between what was once Arab civilization at its height and today's cultural desert.

A 2002 report by the United Nations Development Programme provides a chilling illustration.[1] Among Arab nations, 50 percent of women are illiterate. Only 330 books are translated every year in this vast part of the world. This is three times fewer than in the single, relatively small country of Greece, which itself is hardly a model of present greatness, suffering as it does from the same identity syndrome of a meager contemporary culture as compared to the glory of its founders who, 2,500 years ago, produced a culture that has survived to remind today's Greeks of their origins.

Furthermore, the gross national product of all the Arab countries combined (oil producers included) is less than that of Spain. To the cultural vacuum is added a shortage of material production. This double shortfall has led stakeholders and driving forces to emigrate to countries where unfulfilled and frustrated young people can realize their ambitions. The evidence is incontrovertible: Arabs thrive once they leave their home countries and settle north of the Mediterranean or across the Atlantic, whether in a Latin or Anglo-Saxon context. Despite the legacy of adversity, despite the inequalities and obstacles specific to the host countries, the elite of this diaspora prosper in everything from capital investment to manual labor, from intellectual work to creative ventures.

We are thus faced with this paradox that compels us to conclude that within Arab countries themselves, there is very little participation in the great intellectual ventures of our time, in its landmark inventions. This same Arab world is obviously capable of producing high-performance individuals who, in the universities and research labs of Europe and America, are delving into their own history while taking on subjects and issues that make a difference in human destiny. Others excel in workshops and studios in the West, and still others make a name in the performing arts. In other words, Arab excellence seems to blossom abroad.

From Morocco to Iraq, in this early twenty-first century, there exists not a single research institution worthy of that name. As I see it, there is nothing to stimulate a true, grassroots movement to adapt to the contemporary age. Iraq alone might have succeeded in this ambition, one that was perverted and subverted by its own aggressive ideology. We know how that story turned out: the military-industrial and totalitarian orientation of a bellicose and hegemonic regime brought about the self-destruction of a country, which the calamitous American war only served to hasten and complete.

A similar realization has begun to dawn within the Arab countries. King Abdullah, then still prince and heir apparent to the Saudi throne (though managing the country, in effect), questioned his counterparts at the annual meeting of heads of state of the Arabian peninsula (this was autumn 2001, soon after the 9/11 attacks): "Our populations are large, our territory vast, and money is not lacking. Why do we then have so little power? Why do we not have the means to act upon anything, or even to affect the future of our region?"

There can be little doubt that this dire situation springs from the nature of the regimes in power, which feature various degrees of despotism, tyranny, dictatorship, and denial of basic rights to their populations.

In the case of Saudi Arabia, it is worth recalling the role of fanatical preachers, whose influence must not be downplayed. It is no coincidence that the man who inspired the 9/11 attacks, as well as the fifteen who carried them out, were Saudis.

The Saudi monarchy, it bears repeating, is based on Wahhabism, which presents an extremely schematic and inflexible vision of Islam.[2] This radical form of monotheism refuses any kind of questioning that might humanize the terror of the Absolute. In this version of Islam, God is absent, unknown and unknowable, reduced to a sterile abstraction. All inner experience is therefore banned, any form of intercession abolished. There is no longer any place for the uneasy splendor handed down by the spiritual masters. Nor is any legitimacy granted to popular forms of religiosity expressed through the Dionysian theatricality of the veneration of saints. Everything relished by metaphysicians and anthropologists is ostracized. The wealth of vernacular tradition is swept aside by a standardization that imposes doctrines that conserve only Law and worship, by norms that require conformity. All this results in a stifling social censorship exerted by morals squads that police people's everyday lives in a most ostentatious manner, in order to maintain the patriarchal order built on the revocation of any alternative, and the confinement of minorities and women to a blatantly inferior status in daily affairs.

Wahhabism is probably the most impoverished interpretation known in the theological and doctrinal history of Islam. According to its outlook, any human activity necessary to build and nourish the imagination and symbolic process, anything involving artistic or literary creativity, is seen as vain, or as a diversion from the rigid prescriptions of worship and the pious life. The rigor of this "orthopraxis" results in a negation of civilization itself. It goes without saying that Muslims could never have produced the brilliant civilization handed down to us if they had lived according to the principles imposed by the Wahhabites. Rather, Muslim civilization, in accordance with the religious principles that underpinned it—a civilization that transformed Civilization itself[3]—was elaborated along several modalities at once. At times, it demonstrated inventiveness in response to the requirements of Law (e.g., the link between algebra and the complex rules of distribution that govern the rights of succession[4]); at other times, it skirted the core principles with bold interpretations (as in Sufism or in philosophy and theology using Greek instruments); and at still other times it simply transgressed the commandments (as in the dense Bacchic poetry and iconography which show that through the mediation of wine, the subjects of Islam merge into a crossroads of civilization where Greece, Persia, Arabia, and the Latin world meet[5]).

But let us leave Islam here, and turn to Arabness, which is a secular idea. What remains today of the grand notion of the Arab nation which, in the mid–nineteenth century, was so promising that the phenomenon was termed *nahdha*, or renaissance, resurrection? It is noteworthy that a significant number of those promoting this Arabness were Christians. This was a way for them to foreground the nation, as opposed to religion, as wellspring of identity.

We now know that Arabism ended in utter failure, for the politicians who took up the cause thought that all they needed to succeed was to strike a populist tone and to dazzle the people with their magical rhetoric. The very idea of "Arab" appears to be a given, which is exactly what makes it so deceptive and misleading, a trap for naive, militant ideologues who lack political culture and technique. Because, as Ernest Renan explains in his 1882 conference paper, *Qu'est-ce qu'une nation?* (What Is a Nation?), a linguistic community, geographic continuity, a shared history, ethnic homogeneity, religious solidarity—all these conditions are still insufficient to constitute a nation. A nation is a spiritual principle, says Renan, that cannot be ensured by race, language, interests, religious affinity, geography, or military necessity.[6] What matters most in nation building is a political will that fulfills the desire to share a common destiny in the here and now, in remembrance of a legacy acknowledged by all. But in the Arab case, political will has expressed itself through entities already in place that gained confirmation by adapting to the structures of the nation-state. Like language, history and geography did not succeed in bringing Arabs together. With the collapse of Arabism, most patently demonstrated by the June 1967 defeat by Israel, the scene was once again vacant and available to receive the utopia of a religiously based community.

In fact, Arabness and Islam represent a false dichotomy. In the 1950s, certain Western powers sought to take advantage of such an opposition by building an allied Islamic axis (the Baghdad Pact) against what they saw as the hostile Arabism of Nasser and the Ba'ath parties of Syria and Iraq. But already, with his characteristic intuition, Albert Camus saw the dichotomy as two sides of the same coin, when observing how they affected the Maghreb:

> The more far-sighted militants of the North African Movement, those who know that the *Arab* future depends entirely on how quickly Muslim peoples accede to the conditions of modern life, seem at times overwhelmed by a movement blinded by the dream of a *Pan-Islamism* that may sound feasible in Cairo, but does not stand up to the scrutiny of history. This dream . . . has no chance of coming true in the near future, which is what makes it so dangerous. Whatever one might think of technical civilization, it is the only one capable of providing a decent life for people of underdeveloped countries. It is not the East that will save the East in the end, but rather the West, which itself will derive nourishment from the civilization of the East.[7]

This analysis was prompted by the conflict that arose in postcolonial Tunisia soon after its emancipation, between the Western-leaning Habib Bourguiba and Salah Ben Youssef, more influenced by the East. At the same time, as it happened, in the name of Pan-Arabism, a war was being waged against the Muslim Brotherhood, the inventors of what we today call Islamism. The purportedly pro-Western Pan-Islamic alternative was activated by the United States until the war against the Soviets in Afghanistan in the 1980s. But Camus's "slip" is a telling one, for, as history has shown, Pan-Arabism and Pan-Islamism have turned out to be interchangeable. What they share is greater than what divides them. The so-called secular character of Pan-Arabism has no philosophical or judicial basis. Religious law gets reined in only when it comes to balancing among ethnic minorities. Pan-Islamism and Pan-Arabism join forces in the exaltation of an alternative, anti-Western, antidemocratic identity fueled by an ideology of totalitarian struggle. This is why the historical pattern of Arabism naturally giving way to Islamism has prevailed since the first oil crisis in 1974—for the two phenomena are fed by the same social and anthropological dynamics.

One other factor appears to be a trick of history. As long as Islamic cities maintained their premodern structures, they continued to host a great ethnic diversity that, whatever else one might think, was supported by *dhimmi* status, which granted recognition and legitimacy to Jews, Christians, and other beliefs springing from the Sabian grab bag. I disagree with the way some in Europe denigrate the status of *dhimmi*, considered as stigmatizing sui generis because it acknowledges the other by humiliating and lowering him, as Jacques Ellul writes in a review of a book that Bat Ye'Or, a British historian of Egyptian origin, devotes to the question.[8] There is something anachronistic about this approach to the question. At a time when the notion of universality was theocentric, the institution of *dhimmi* marked an advance that guaranteed encounters would take place, ones that would produce mixing and exchange, sharing and emulation, seeing to it that each group would be written into the story of the other, despite obstacles that hampered the circulation of references from one community to the other. Even during the colonial era, despite the hierarchy among races, languages, and beliefs, despite foreign domination where the outsider ruled as master, the diversity within cities remained active, against all odds, a joy for the rare few who were lucky enough to experience it.

But this feature of Islam would soon be definitively distorted and routed by both Pan-Islamism and Pan-Arabism, two terms that came to designate the same phenomenon: a turning in on oneself, the rejection of difference, the exclusion of others, all resulting in a gradual disappearance of plural society in the name of exclusionary fanaticism at the expense of Jews and Christians in the Muslim city. And yet the cities of the East were in the process of modernizing according to Western models, which should have capitalized on this predisposition to accept difference. Ideally, this process would have reinforced society's diverse composition by replacing the institution of *dhimmi* with the citizen's right to equality. This basic right would take no account of ethnic distinction, sexual identity, linguistic background, or religious affiliation, allowing citizen subjects to govern themselves, fully capable of distinguishing what is determined by heritage from matters concerning personal choice. Once this "transmutation of values" had taken place, the status of *dhimmi* would no longer be recommended; rather, it would be considered dangerously archaic, and "degrading," to use the term of its stern critic, Jacques Ellul. But this is not what happened, and Pan-Arabism proved destructive to ethnic and linguistic minorities, with Jews, Kurds, Druzes, and Berbers suffering the most. Arabism then yielded to Islamism, which only accelerated the dispersal of these societies' religious minorities, Christians in particular, who could no longer conform to the strictures of *dhimmi* status, however diffuse it had become by then; for human experience shows how historically out of step this arrangement had become in contrast to democracy and the rule of law.

A further failure has to do with the material modernization underway since the early nineteenth century. Colonization and bourgeois imperialism are partly responsible, for Europeans were in no hurry to see a competing economic power emerging at their doorstep.

When, in late nineteenth-century Egypt, academics and engineers sought to pursue the work of their masters by translating scientific manuals, French ones in particular, they came up against the British protectorate authorities, who then ruled to forbid the teaching of science in Arabic, and imposed English as the language of instruction. This had the effect of interrupting the modernization of scientific Arabic, which, until then, had been developing out of notions based in "medieval" sources that were rich in possibilities for adapting to the new scientific approach.[9]

Among several aborted attempts to modernize, the fascination with all things technical certainly played a role, for this prompted mass importation of products without going back to the concepts and theoretical speculation that made such products possible. Any item cut off from the idea that brought it about will remain out of reach. Arabs believed they were capable of reproducing new material goods while remaining faithful to their conservative religious culture. But this same culture loathed any form of innovation, thought to exert a corrupting influence on the spirit of tradition, on its original purity.

So what does it mean to be Arab today? How can Arabs remain connected to the early Islamic scene? Speaking for myself, I maintain my Arabic and Islamic references as traces, not as some mythic origin to be restored in the present. I have made a lifelong project of building my spiritual dwelling at the crossroads of my double genealogy: Arab-Islamic and secular-European. I write in French and am inhabited by Arabic. I put my Arabic to work in French. In an ever-spreading world of mixture and circulation, in this emerging world culture, I bring to the table who I am, what I have made my own, and what I know. One of my raisons d'être is to make available Arabic references to the outside world, to get them into circulation, to give them a chance to enrich and act upon any other work willing to welcome them.

Anyone following the traces of Arabic will discover that it is a vehicle of a superb civilization. There are over four million Arabic-language manuscripts in existence (60,000 in Greek, 400,000 in Latin). Many of these manuscripts have never been studied or published. There is enough material to fuel the work of generations of researchers, poets, and thinkers still concerned with the ancient, even in their ultramodern projects of today. For, like Greek and Latin texts, the Arabic writings of old conserve their powerful pertinence for anyone who works at them assiduously. I count these Arab writers of times past among the dead with whom I am in constant dialogue.

With regard to Arab writers today, I often read them with a great sense of unease, for they have forgotten their tradition, while producing poor imitations of the West. Nothing is left of that dialogue with the dead, yet new paths remain unexplored. Of course, many Arab authors have now been translated into several languages and participate in the current trend of world literature. But if I take the case of the novel, I see no prose to equal the oldest available written testimony of *A Thousand and One Nights* as it appears throughout the manuscript transcribed in the fourteenth century, acquired by translator Antoine Galland (1650–1714), and conserved in the French National Library.[10] In this text, a strange alchemy is at work that chooses with great tact between two language registers: The high literary and the lowly vernacular seem to alternate in perfect balance. Between grammar and parataxis, they produce contrasts that lend the stories that verve so absent among today's prose writers, where I see no sign of a leading light in the tradition of last century's Proust, Joyce, Tanizaki, Faulkner, or Kafka.

But the Arab world, beyond its rather grim present, still conserves an enormous human potential among the men and women of its vast territory, where a language and the vestiges of a glorious past remain vital. All that is missing are the political will and the intellectual groundwork to make this potential a reality. Let us first summarize the historical contribution of the Arabs, an intellectual exercise that leaves no room for melancholy or nostalgia when it comes to scrutinizing this vast legacy. It is this legacy that must first be interiorized, then surpassed, before opening onto a more cosmopolitan future. The first step involves the choice of a Westernization that takes account of the idiosyncrasies of the Islamic subject, whose traces have not yet been brought into the conversation currently underway.

CHAPTER 4

## Civilization or Extinction

Islam is a civilization and a religion, but with political ambitions. Today, the first two attributes have been eclipsed by the violence of seditious factions that perpetrate their crimes in Islam's name. The shocking attacks of September 11, 2001, were committed in the name of *jihād*, sometimes translated as "holy war," which had been the historical vector of Islamic expansion. But the question is this: Is the reactivation of *jihād* by today's terrorists theologically legitimate? Are these two forms of *jihād* comparable, and can the same criteria of analysis be applied to the expression of holy war past and present? It is crucial to expose the way today's fundamentalists distort the notion and, in doing so, remove it from the age in which it was forged, tracing it down to the present while ignoring historical changes and major shifts in ideas. It is easy to demonstrate that *jihād*, in theological tradition, is subject to very particular conditions that are not present in the reality of September 11.[1]

Furthermore, even when interpreting dogmatically, though more according to the spirit than the letter of the text, it is possible to infer that this warlike notion belongs to the circumstantial set of divine prescriptions that a certain historical evolution can invalidate. Starting in the mid–nineteenth century, two generations of theologians tended to consider the notion of *jihād* obsolete, while more recent doctrinaire fundamentalists began reestablishing it, around the mid–twentieth century, in order to mobilize recruits for the war of beliefs.

Yet the fundamentalists' actions serve only to confirm the most prevalent vision people have of Islam today, according to which it is by its very nature a bellicose, hegemonic, conquering, and politically violent religion. It is commonly held to be a religion that dares to provoke hostilities even when in a position of inferiority as compared to the more powerful enemies it designates for itself. Faced with this unfavorable balance of power, rather than renouncing war, it adopts terrorist tactics that turn it into a formidable foe capable of doing great harm. Those who engage in such acts are all the more intimidating in that they are prepared to die in order to honor the myth of sacrifice, offering up their lives in an act of holy destruction.

The events of September 11 remain in the forefront of world consciousness and demand of all humanity an all-out struggle against fundamentalist terror. This struggle is both a challenge and a test for democracy. In addition to the overt war on terror that consists of tracking the mobile hideouts of armed Islamist militants, we must not lose sight of the far more subtle and slow-moving angle of attack involving the judicial process that will thwart members of so-called sleeper cells that lead an otherwise ordinary existence in societies based on freedom of speech, assembly, movement, and enterprise. Faced with this threat, we must curb our impatience. For it is often during extreme times that the force of law is put to the test, particularly those laws that provide for an extension of their authority in exceptional situations.

But my purpose here is not to inquire as to what ought to be tested. Rather, I wish to state that such high-profile incidents blur our understanding of Islam as a complex historical phenomenon. They blind us to its potential, to its full range of possibilities, and confirm the stereotypes that place it in the position of enemy. This biased view of Islam is in fact the best ally of someone like Osama Bin Laden, and his acolytes and henchmen. One way to fight against fundamentalism, therefore, is to acknowledge Islam in all its complexity and its contributions to universal culture. And the best way to accomplish this is to avoid reducing it to its mere political and warmongering expression, and to view it first of all as a civilization and a religion, before dealing with its political and expansionist vocation.

When speaking of Islamic civilization, I wish first of all to temper the particularist tendency that this term evokes, and rather to address an issue shared by us all, beyond the formal and linguistic specificities that distinguish the contributions of each nation and people, establishing difference and illustrating human diversity across time and space. I would like to move beyond two ways of apprehending the world, one of which carries some truth, with the other representing a widespread prejudice.

The first seeks to circumscribe the contours of identity upon which civilizations are built. Thus, we proceed to study the Chinese, Indian, Amerindian, or Egyptian civilizations, locating their birth, growth, golden age, decline, and, in some cases, the very moment of their demise.

The second concerns the vision that already constituted communities project upon other communities: When we look at other civilizations, we tend to deem only our own as truly civilized and to reject the others as barbarous. I would hope that we could get beyond both of these approaches (which associate partial truth and cliché) by integrating the notion of *internal* tension between civilization and barbarity within each human establishment. It is this tension that produces the creative energy necessary for great works. Here, plurality is converted into singularity. Civilizations feed on a singular civilizing principle, always threatened by the aggression of barbarity, and history has taught us that no gains, however permanent they may appear, can deliver Man from this destructive attraction. In short, the civilizing act emanating from one civilization or another nourishes *civilization* in the broader sense, which is threatened by the barbarity that lies deep within the very ones that invent and build. Where the civilizing act requires effort, abnegation, and reaching beyond limits, barbarity corresponds to instinct and the natural state, the conclusion reached by Freud in his *Civilization and Its Discontents.* In short, the tension between Eros and Thanatos lurks within each of us, ready to act and to fan the flames of civil war that Man can spark at any moment.

The best illustration of this conclusion occurred in the mid–twentieth century, when one of the most advanced peoples of modern, European, Western civilization gave rise to Nazism, a dark and lethal barbarity allied with technology, what Heidegger termed "the end of metaphysics." If we are to trust the vision of the great Arab historian Ibn Khaldūn (fourteenth c.)[2], we conclude that this swing between civilization and barbarity is the motor that turns the wheels of history in the territories of Islam, down through all states and dynasties. This thinker developed a cyclical vision of history, a kind of eternal return whereby the civilization of cities is fated to perish, to collapse back into barbarity. Warring strongholds emanating from tribal and nomadic territories first harass, then invade the cities and destroy them. Then, these new arrivals, having initiated their ascension by a barbarous act, settle into the remains of the civilization they have just destroyed and slowly begin to rebuild. They in turn become civilized, build and expand, and finally perish, soon to be replaced by their conquerors who start out as barbarians, grow into a civilization, and fall into decadence. . . . Each is thus destined to go through the same stages in endless, relentless succession.

I would now like to illustrate the civilizing effects of Islam in the same perspective. What I posit is simple and straightforward: Islam at its peak brought to the world a level of civilization theretofore unknown. To support this argument, I will need to situate Islam in the time and place of its genesis and development. There are two opposing viewpoints in this respect: the one defended by Henri Pirenne in his *Mahomet et Charlemagne*,[3] who believes that the rise of Islam on the Mediterranean scene marked an irreparable break; and that of Maurice Lombard in his book *L'Islam dans sa première grandeur*,[4] who emphasizes the continuity of the civilizing effects of Islamic authority, at least during the period lasting from the eighth to the eleventh centuries.

It should be obvious that I support the thesis of continuity, and I will have no trouble illustrating it with multiple examples.

I begin with architecture for, as Viollet-le-Duc put it, architecture is the "mirror of ideology." Its mix of forms says a great deal about the people who live in and among its edifices.. The great monuments of Islam were able to adapt their new cultural constraints to the grand architectural traditions of the recently conquered lands of declining antiquity. The Dome of the Rock (692) in Jerusalem represents the culminating point of a process begun in the sixth century B.C. It is the perfect realization of the central plan idea inaugurated by the orchestra of the Greek theater, carried through to the treasures of Delphi, the circular temples of Rome, and the early Christian and Byzantine churches built on the octagonal model or centered on the Greek cross.[5] Elsewhere, the Umayyad Mosque of Damascus (c. 710) represents the perfect illustration of the Roman basilica plan, with its three lofty parallel naves.

Naturally, the inherited forms are subject to the requirements of the new religion since, in all the examples just mentioned, the monuments intended for worship visualize their orientation toward Mecca by means of the *mihrab*, the small alcove that points toward the Kaaba, the cube draped in black cloth, the omphalos of the world, located at the center of the sacred enclosure, the point faced by all believers in prayer, and around which they circumambulate when on their pilgrimage to the holy city.

The decor is also adapted to these new requirements. Without banning all iconic representation in the place of worship, the Prophet's recommendation to limit representation to inanimate objects was respected, and thus the Byzantine mosaics were stripped of their animate beings, both humans and beasts. In Jerusalem, the decor was thus reduced to geometric and floral patterns, both emblematic and epigraphic. In Damascus, landscapes associate stately architecture with tree-lined gardens in bloom and flowing rivers, which some have identified as imitating the Koranic paradise, the shaded grove that fulfills the dream of the desert dweller subjected to the punishing sun.

It is worth focusing a moment on the monumental letters that shine from the walls of the Jerusalem rotunda, for they testify to a far-reaching inaugural act. These letters attest first of all to the building's date (A.H. 72 , or A.D. 692). They also display one of the oldest Koranic transcriptions. And last, they represent a transfer of writing to a monumental scale, from parchment to wall, calligraphy in stone. Calligraphy being Islam's first art, it is intended to exalt the letter, the incarnation of the voice, the divine Word, and thus refers to the realm of the symbolic, on same order as do the Tablets in Jewish tradition and the body of Christ in Christianity.[6]

And if we take the example of the ninth-century mosques of the Muslim west, those of al-Qairawān and al-Zaytūna in Tunis, we will note that the builders of these vast hypostyle halls drew materials from their Roman and Byzantine antecedents, as if they were quarries or workshops churning out columns and capitals. This might be interpreted as plundering, a will to negate the Roman temple or the Byzantine basilica. But the archaeological record proves otherwise, for when the Arabs arrived in Africa near the end of the seventh century, not only were most of the monumental ensembles no longer functioning, but they had been abandoned, had fallen into disrepair, what we would today call ruins. Their reuse thus gave new life to an abandoned sign. A form of emulation comes into play, whereby those who borrow feel they must live up to the standards of the objects they are investing with new meaning, sometimes within the very walls of the former edifices.

The new user might sometimes wish to surpass the former by designing a space on a different scale meant to honor the ornament that had served differently elsewhere.

Apart from their intrinsic beauty, these two mosques—that of al-Qairawān in particular—constitute two museums of Roman and Byzantine columns and capitals. These are so numerous and varied that they offer precious examples that allow us an important insight into the commerce of marble and the way it was processed all over the Mediterranean at that time. Thus, by virtue of random recycling of the artifacts of antiquity, Islamic monuments played a role in the conservation of certain sectors of empire, of both Rome and Constantinople.

If works produced in the lands of Islam are not necessarily continuous with former empires, they still involve these ancient references. Civilizations do not invent ex nihilo, but rather by mixing. A further example of this phenomenon is provided by another outstanding mosque, that of Cordova, which has been a source of fascination for countless visitors over the centuries. Among the many, let me cite Edgar Quinet, who, in the winter of 1844, remarked upon the "thousand columns . . . mingled with the abandon of primeval nature."[7] Or Rainer Maria Rilke, in one of his letters, where he castigates the Catholic intrusion that breaks up the building's flow.[8]

This forest of columns, completed in the tenth century, is the metaphor of an oasis that, like its desert model in Africa, reproduces the play of light and shadow of a palm grove. It is a *tenebrae* that celebrates the yearning for the place of origin experienced by the Arab in exile, far from the land of his forebears. Each column fans out to create arches, the metaphoric palm, that tree favored among all others that was brought along and acclimated to the gardens of Andalusia, like the one that prompted an improvised verse from the Umayyad prince 'Abderrahmān the Émigré,[9] who in 750 escaped the massacre of his people by the Abbasids in the bloodied waters of the Euphrates. He would go on to settle on the banks of the Guadalquivir to revive the fallen dynasty that, some 150 years later, would claim to embody the very spirit of the imperial caliphate.

This Cordova mosque, founded by the same 'Abderrahmān, testifies to that imperial glory. The reuse of ancient columns here is manifest, and the Roman stonework of the Segovia aqueduct inspired the double layers of arches (not unlike those of the earlier Umayyad mosque of Damascus, built in 710 by the Caliph Walīd II). The *Basileus* in person sent the caliph a team of mosaic craftsmen to decorate the wall that would house the recessed *mihrab* and vault.[10] All eyes are drawn to this dazzling jewel, where gold, silver, azure, and emerald fairly ring out. The crossing of ogival arches is employed to splendid effect, a feature that would later be adopted in countries to the north, where Gothic structures would make use of it as a basic structuring element.

This mosque, the quintessence of Islamic art, thus represents Arab nostalgia embodied in a structure that uses art pieces from antiquity that infuse the new edifice with Roman reminiscences. At its focal point, it exudes Byzantine luxuriance, and viewers can easily see forward to the Gothic period, and even through to the Baroque, in its vaulting and dome structures. The profile of the cupolas, combined with the ogival crossings, captures light in certain of their openings, creating geometrical light patterns that will be found seven centuries later in the Church of San Lorenzo in Turin, a mid–seventeenth-century edifice by Guarino Guarini.[11]

At a time when Europe was moving away from its Greco-Roman sources, Islam provided continuity. The baths so common in antiquity were adapted as hammams, so numerous in all the cities of Islam (and walled up by the Christians throughout the reconquest of Andalusian cities such as Cordova. In that city, in the early thirteenth century, the first act of the new Catholic authorities was to forbid access to the nearly three hundred public baths operating in the city at that time, an act that Nietzsche took as emblematic of traditional Christianity's "nihilism" of the body.[12])

It was Islam's purification rites that allowed Roman baths not only to survive but to thrive, reviving these ancient structures where hot water and steam circulate through brick channels distributed all along the rooms, whose function depends on distance and flow, from hotter to colder. Arab baths emulated the Roman division of space into dressing room (*apoditarium*), cool room (*frigidarium*), warm room (*tepidarium*), and hot room (*caldarium*).

It is also possible to trace the continuity of Roman influences in two other works, which might at first be perceived as radically different.

What is more antithetical, at first glance, than the rigor of Roman urbanism and the apparent anarchy of Islamic cities? One corresponds to an obsession with the orthogonal ideal, while the other is a labyrinth that would confound even Ariadne. On the one hand, roads that cross at perfect right angles; on the other, dense thickets of paths that appear randomly drawn. I will spare the reader the inept conclusions that have been drawn from this comparison, ones that attribute geometric reason to the masters of the grid, and the disorder of improvisation to those whose mazelike cities seem designed to mislead strangers unable to distinguish throughways from dead ends, not to mention the anxiety experienced when one is obliged to break stride, stop, and retrace one's steps after walking into one of those impasses.

The true structure of the Islamic city is more complex than that. For one, the functional principles of Roman urbanism are in fact quite discernible. It's just that the master builders of Islam refuse to systematize them. Every city is based on the axes of *cardo* and *decumanus*, which often run parallel, then snake around to reach city gates that correspond to the four cardinal points. At their central meeting place, a forum-like space incorporates the place of worship and markets, including both merchants and artisans, along with a palace or citadel in some cases. Very often, the vast courtyard of the city's great mosque serves as a public square, a feature found in the Umayyad

Mosque of Damascus, the Azhar in Cairo, the Zaytūna in Tunis, and the Qarawīn in Fez. Around this basic Roman layout, the maze branches out in clusters composed of units that originally adhered to the same esprit de corps—tribe, clan, clientele—that founded the logic of neighborhoods on a communitarian basis. All historic cities in the southern rim of the Mediterranean function according to this double reference, which lends the improvisation ascribed to tribal, clan, or ethnic solidarity a structuring function, inspired by Roman urban principles. This paradoxical duality is a permanent feature of all cities built between the eighth and seventeenth centuries, and determines the urban network, whether it be in Fez, Rabat, Marrakesh, Tunis, Cairo, Damascus, or Aleppo.

The second example that converts Islamic foreignness into Roman familiarity is most certainly the house.[13] What differentiates the Arab house is its blind facade, preventing the outsider from seeing in. The only opening onto the street, the door, is itself a barrier to curious eyes in that it opens into a long, zigzagging corridor. This arrangement reinforces the inwardness that houses in Islam are famous for, along with the reputation for a strict separation between public and private space, further emphasized by the veiling codes affecting women's face, hair, limbs, and so on that need protection from the eyes of strangers.

But once inside one of these domestic dwellings, one discovers that the basic structure is built according to a Roman layout centered on a portico that opens onto a courtyard, with a walled garden extending beyond one of the built wings, a second opening to the blue sky above. What's more, once the Italian cities of the Renaissance began making archaeological reference to Rome, they started including courtyards in their patrician dwellings, giving them a surprising resemblance to their counterparts on the southern shore.

Finally, I shall evoke what might be termed the civilization of villas, which experienced a hiatus in Christian Europe but a continuity in Islam. All the grand families of Cordova owned an *intro-muros* city dwelling and a villa outside the city, particularly in the hillside regions. Chronicles report this trend, which is often confirmed by archaeological vestiges found in areas around Rusafa, Madīnat az-Zahrā', and Madīnat az-Zāhira, a short distance from Cordova, an agglomeration located on a branch where the Guadalquivir opens up.

A major literary work, *The Ring of the Dove,* written around the year 1000 by a resident of Cordova, Ibn Hazm, tells of the yearly migration of families in high summer to their pleasure estates, where the air is fresher and breezes cool the evenings, while back in the city, soaring summer temperatures stifle the tightly woven urban fabric where brick and stone retain the daytime heat, making even the night air impossible to breathe.[14]

Agricultural treatises, like that of Saʻd Ibn Luyūn (1282–1349), native of Almeria, describe in detail the way space is distributed in these estates.[15] Barns, stables, and chicken coops are the most remote from the villa, followed by the vegetable garden, then the fruit groves, and finally, nearest to the master dwelling, the flowerbeds separated by cooling pools and fountains that provide the music of flowing water as it cascades from one pool to the next, to the delight of the summering families and their guests.

These Andalusian estates are halfway between the Roman villa and the Renaissance pleasure homes built by the grand families of Tuscany and the Veneto. The distribution of space described by Ibn Luyūn bears a strong resemblance to that which tested the talents of Palladio, who made use of it time and again for the villas he built along the Brenta, in the backcountry of Padua, the environs of Vicenza, or the outskirts of Treviso.

And speaking of agricultural treatises with regard to villas, I might cite the most famous of them all, the one composed in the thirteenth century by a Seville native, Ibn al-ʻAwwām.[16] This work tells us first that agriculture was considered at once a science, a technique, an art, and a craft. The book is the product of a number of inputs—Babylonian, Greek, Roman, Syrian, Byzantine, Iberian—supported by an experimental method.

This manner of fusion is what created the new spirit of civilization that prospered in the name of Islam. In this civilization, traditions that had been isolated from one another came together and thrived.

The principle of continuity involves not only the Greco-Roman traditions but those of both East and West that merged in this crucible, giving rise to the true civilization of Islam. Ensuring the continuity of a tradition, assuming a cultural legacy, does not imply the submission of disciple to master, or to conservative values. Like a trained expert who can draw a synthesis from a general overview, the Arab genius involved continuity but with a critical, pragmatic approach that stimulated invention. We will see later how the sciences developed in Arabic confirmed this principle.

As stated above, the work of architectural invention within the Western tradition implies the possibility of continuity with other traditions as well, notably those of the East. Proof of this can be found among the vestiges of Persian civilization, one example being the monumental vault of the Sassanid palace of Ctesiphon (sixth c.), which would go on to serve as a model for *iwān* architecture, applied universally in Islamic cities, starting in Mesopotamia and spreading east and west, from Egypt to India. The *iwān* is a lofty vaulted space, walled on three sides, with one end opening to its full height onto a courtyard.

This Eastern emulation brings to the Islamic oratory the conquest of height usually suggestive of the religious experience of ascension, the journey of the spirit heavenward toward the celestial spheres. Transcendence is thus visualized through the mastery of elevation. Conversely, the Western mosques mentioned earlier illustrate in their horizontality a religious notion that brings heaven closer to earth and grants immanent presence to transcendence.

One of the more beautiful realizations of this *iwān* feature is the Mamlūk *medersa* built in Cairo by Sultan Hassan (early fourteenth c.). The local fifteenth-century chronicler, Maqrīzī, reveals in his *Khitat* that the shared purpose of architect and sponsor was to rival the Sassanid model, both technically and aesthetically, by surpassing the monumental Ctesiphon vault by five cubits.[17]

Another invention that took an ancient masterwork as its model comes from Ottoman architecture, wherein the ingenious Sinan, in the sixteenth century, emulated the work of Anthemius of Tralles and Isidore of Miletus, the architects commissioned to design the church of Hagia Sophia (532–37), which would constitute the third grand model followed by mosque architecture, along with the *iwān* and the hypostyle, basilica spaces. Not content to merely imitate the Hagia Sophia, Sinan drew on its full potential for inspiration, exhausting every possibility.

From among his profuse and ever-evolving oeuvre, I will cite one of his earlier works, the Şehzade Mosque (1548) in Istanbul, where the architect departed slightly from the model by setting four semidomes around the central dome, itself built into a square plan. And since the height of the dome (37.5 meters) is nearly identical to the side of the square (38 meters), the interior volume gives the illusion of a cube, the form to which Plato ascribed "eternal beauty." The cloverleaf of half-domes set into the square responds to the square of the courtyard, thereby applying the Pythagorean arrangement of "squares turning in a circle."[18] As always with Sinan, the slightest detail is designed with utmost care and contributes to the overall dynamics, so that the removal of any single element would disturb its unity.

With his references to Platonism, his Greek spirit of geometry, his taste for monumentality, his extremely precise draftsmanship, and his concern for movement in unity (also a feature of Alberti), Sinan's experience provides a superb counterpart to that of his elder by one generation, Michelangelo. In both instances, the myth of architect as demiurge is embodied, East and West, via these two nearly contemporary figures.

It hardly seems appropriate to continue talking about the categories of East and West when there is so much overlap on either side. It makes more sense to situate Islamic architecture,

if not in a shared European history, then at least in a diachronic perspective, certainly distinct in many ways but that
has crisscrossed the Mediterranean in all directions, enriching
as much as it was enriched.

Remaining in the realm of architecture, I note a further example of another moment in Islamic art that is contempora-
neous with a Western project, again having to do with the
articulation of the cube and the dome, and the geometrical issues
involved. Around the 1420s, this articulation was being made
manifest in Florentine works by Brunelleschi (the sacristy of
San Lorenzo, the Pazzi chapel of the Santa Croce basilica, Santa
Maria degli Angeli). Meanwhile, in 1424 in Bursa, the first capital of the Ottomans, the Yeşil Cami was built, the so-called
Green Mosque, which, with a central hall, two lateral rooms,
and an entry space, offers four resolutions to the same set of
problems that were challenging the Tuscan Quattrocento's first
generation.

The archives tell us that Brunelleschi was typical of artists
whose works were always preceded by theoretical speculations.
We can state as much for the designer of the Green Mosque by
virtue of this one realization, since he posits several solutions to
the same problem in a single monument, as if the resulting
work were nothing but the illustration of a dissertation con-
taining meditations on pure geometry.

This relation of cube to sphere was worked out by Greek
geometers, and further developed by their Arab successors,
who produced treatises on applied geometry (*Le Livre des constructions géométriques necessaires à l'artisan* by Abū al-Wafā'
al-Buzjāni, tenth century).[19] The collaboration between geometric and architectural knowledge deals with the same issue in
Byzantine, Coptic, and Visigoth churches from the fifth century
onward.

My point here is not to deny Brunelleschi's originality, but
rather to confirm the approach of a Renaissance man who
sought to revive the Greco-Roman tradition, based upon the
archaeological record. With regard to the master of the Green

Mosque, we can state that he also belongs to a culture that never broke the link with antiquity.

Such comparisons clearly demonstrate that all these cultural signs are circulating in a single geographic and imaginative space: the Mediterranean. With these two examples coming from the 1420s, we have undeniable evidence that the continuity of ancient references remained unbroken within Islam, while the break in Europe required the fresh ideology of the Renaissance for a return to the ancient fundaments.

We shall complete this retracing exercise by broadening the field, from architecture to sculpture, for a time remaining in Florence in the company of Brunelleschi. He was among the participants in a competition launched by the city to select the artist to decorate the baptistery doors, facing the facade of Santa Maria del Fiore. The subject of one panel, the sacrifice of Abraham, is one of the most familiar to memory nourished by Islamic rites. It was as if this choice of subject had been intended to facilitate the encounter with Islamic references for Ghiberti, the famous metalworker and sculptor who eventually won the commission. He had studied optics by reading al-Kindī (eleventh c.), whom he respectfully cites, and especially Ibn al-Haytham (eleventh c.), known in Europe by his surname, Alhazen.[20]

In his *De Optica*, Ibn al-Haytham devotes a chapter to perception (*al-Idrāk*), which he subjects to the conditions of twenty-one categories, enriching the Ptolemaic legacy (distance, movement, light, color, speed, smoothness, roughness, etc.). Beside the analysis of perception as a physical, mental, and psychic phenomenon, the whole point comes down to aesthetic discernment, the distinction between ugly and beautiful, the ultimate categories that become the raison d'être of all perception. All the other categories are deployed as a function of these two, offering a relativist aesthetic vision. Among many reference points, measure, or "balanced proportion" (*tanāsub*), and harmony (*al-i'tilāf*) among parts of a whole, together can characterize the beautiful.[21] This is the art of proportion inherited from the Platonist and Pythagorean traditions, divulged to the craftsmen of Islam via the Neoplatonist and Pythagorean encyclopedia compiled for their education, the epistles of the Brothers of Purity (*Rasā'il ikhwān aç-Çafā*, tenth c.).[22] It was this criterion of proportion that Ghiberti appropriated as the basis for his notion of beauty.[23]

The epistemologist and historian of science Gérard Simon demonstrates in a recent book that the revolution of visual perception set in motion by Ibn al-Haytham explains the terms in which the question of perspective would later be formulated, both as a technical problem of pure geometry and as "symbolic form," to use Panofsky's expression.[24] Thus, perspective, the very basis of the revolution that gave the pictorial art of Europe its identity, cannot be explained without the mediation of a work written by a scholar living in eleventh-century Islam, writing in Arabic, and translated into Latin in the twelfth century. This analytical direction is further explored by Hans Belting in a work that compares the link between science and art at two moments of intellectual and civilizational upheaval: Baghdad in the ninth to eleventh centuries, and Florence in the fifteenth and sixteenth centuries.[25]

Before returning to this effect of optics on the arts in both East and West, let us observe that, according to Gérard Simon, the history of classic optics is conceived diachronically, with first of all the Greek beginnings in two stages, that of Euclid (fourth c. B.C.) and of Ptolemy (second c.), and then the intermediary Arab period represented by the breakthrough of Ibn al-Haytham (eleventh c.), and finally the passage out of Latin into modern European languages, with authors such as Copernicus, Descartes, and Malebranche, who all followed in the footsteps of Ibn al-Haytham. The next new turn in the history of optics would take place only with Newton and his work on the spectrum.

The case of Ibn al-Haytham seems exemplary with regard to references shared between East and West. His work was kept alive and vital from the eleventh through the sixteenth centuries,

from its translation into Latin by Vitellion (twelfth c.) to its
publication by Frederico Risnero in Basel in 1572. Let us first
retrace the man's beginnings, for a return to his career rectifies
the conventional vision we have of the Arabs' connection to the
Greeks. The Arabs served as something more than mere trans-
mitters: They were also active readers and critics who worked at
enriching, extending, and refining the works of antiquity, and
in so doing moved science forward, sometimes changing its
course. This is manifest in Ibn al-Haytham's relation to the
works of Euclid and Ptolemy, at the crossroads where optics,
geometry, and astronomy converge. One of Ibn al-Haytham's
treatises is a close critical reading of Ptolemy in which he subjects theory to mathematical reasoning and experimentation,
and ends up either refuting or refining him, after passing judgment on large sections of the *Almageste*, the treatise on the
movement of heavenly bodies or scrutinizing other of his pieces
on optical illusion and mirrors, in connection with reflection
and refraction.[26]

Let us return to the effect that Ibn al-Haytham had on the
visual arts, East and West, for it was his oeuvre and the body of
work it engendered that gave rise to both Islamic and European methods of representation, however remote these might
seem from one another, based as they are in quite distinct, or
even antithetical, philosophical and ontological principles.
The two forms of Islamic ornament par excellence, arabesques
and stalactites, or *muqarnaça*, issue from the same geometric
patterns that illustrate the concept of optical illusion. The ki-
netics of these forms creates a chasm within the flat, two-
dimensional surface or the three-dimensional arrangement,
causing observers to doubt what they see and inducing a delightful dizziness.

Perspective, which flourished during the Tuscan Quattrocento, after some earlier, hesitant strides in the Trecento,
owes much to the *Opticae thesaurus Alhazeni Arabis*, Ibn
al-Haytham's optics manual which, as I mentioned above,
exerted such a strong influence on Ghiberti in matters of pro-

portion. The Arab scholar devoted numerous remarks, analyses, and experiments to phenomena of optical illusion with respect to the whole process of perception. Four of the many categories he enumerated have to do with perspective: light, color and distance (which he categorizes as concerning atmospheric perspective), and speed (which transforms the visible size of objects and is categorized as movement perspective). Ibn al-Haytham even invented a kind of kinetoscope, a circle with alternating holes and opaque spaces that turned around a little statue of a horse which then seemed to be galloping. For light, he built his own camera obscura, reconstituted in the museum in Frankfurt devoted to Arab-Islamic sciences.[27] Form and meaning (*çūra* and *ma'nā*) join to organize the geometric patterns that create depth of field and perspective, which then procure the illusion of a third dimension on a surface where only two exist. This play of illusion goes so far as to include "tricks of the eye" (*aghlāt al-baçar*), to which Ibn al-Haytham devotes his third dissertation involving experiments and geometrical analysis, the same one used by the painters and architects who founded mathematical perspective in Florence, such as Masaccio, whose fresco devoted to the Trinity followed Brunelleschi's lead.[28] This pictorial work stands as a manifesto in favor of the new way of representing space in painting. Ibn al-Haytham dealt with the issue of visual illusions in connection with light (and color, as opposed to darkness), movement (at varying speeds), and distance (favoring the median segment that frames the visible field, limited at its extremes by a threshold of invisibility that determines the close and the distant). Beyond the principles of perspective, all these processes converge upon different ways of achieving trompe-l'oeil and anamorphosis in Western painting.

It is actually astonishing that the same reference to Ibn al-Haytham could have produced two such distinct and dissimilar visual orders. The West, by universalizing perspective, opted for an illusion that seeks to account for something real. It is perhaps reassuring that this move from one scene to another has come to symbolize the energy that has led to the West's conquest of matter. At the nexus of science, art, and technology, Man's grasp of the real facilitated action to transform it. Conversely, when the spirit of geometry is turned primarily toward ornament, as was the case in the East, the result is an abstraction that, when contemplated, troubles the senses and procures a heady pleasure experienced in a state of immobility, of inaction. The field of vision vibrates as it captures the real behind the moving grid that veils and shifts reality through these high-speed kinetic effects, produced by networks of arabesques such as star-shaped polygons and stalactites.

The example of Ibn al-Haytham's effects on the arts of East and West also holds true for the sciences. The same ideas encountered with regard to art and architecture will appear again, but even more clearly, as we follow the development of the sciences in Arabic, mathematics in particular. The prevailing view with regard to mathematics in Arabic used to consist of three main contributions: making Arabic numerals universal, discovering algebra, and transmitting to the West the Greek tradition (Euclid, Apollonius, Archimedes, Diophantine, etc.). But this view has come to appear increasingly limited ever since Roshdi Rashed's research into this field started to gain notoriety.[29]

It has now been established that in ninth-century Baghdad, a major shift in the history of mathematics took place due to the convergence, via translation, of traditions that until then had not come together: Within Arabic, there merged the legacies of the Egyptians, Persians, Indians, and, as has recently come to light, the Chinese.[30] On the basis of these encounters, differences and syntheses gave way to the elaboration of a new way of thinking about science.

Let us focus for a moment on the work of al-Khwārizmī, who brought about the invention of algebra,[31] which reflects accurately on the cultural and intellectual climate of a Baghdad that was both productive and receptive. This new *mathesis*, which posited a mathematical discipline different from both arithmetic and geometry, but capable of mobilizing each for its own ends, also corresponds to a new scientific spirit that issues not only from the mathematical disciplines but also from other sciences such as those of linguists and jurists, including the combinatory principle. Al-Khalīl Ibn Ahmad (718–86), a mathematician and musicologist, was also the founder of Arabic-language phonology, prosody, and morphology. In these areas, notably in lexicography and prosody, he developed an exhaustive a priori classification whose process is combinatory. "Here is where al-Khalīl elaborates the theory that can be summed up thus: language is a phonetically realized part of the possible language. The words of this possible language are obtained by the combination and permutation of letters. The phonetically realized part consists of those words of the possible language that verify the rules of phonetic compatibility and are effectively used. The lexicographer is thus faced with two tasks at once: one deliberately and solely combinatory, and the other phonological."[32] The same steps are applied to prosody. Men of science at the time had perceived in this combinatory approach a calculus (*hisāb*). "This new methodology is also a new epistemology that conveys an idea of science different from the one inherited from Hellenistic tradition. . . . It is this same conception of science and its object, underpinned by the same method, that is found in the book of al-Khwārizmī, and which would spread to other areas of mathematics, in both algebra and geometry, and number theory."[33]

The other area of research taken into consideration by al-Khwārizmī is the calculations by jurists with regard to cases of inheritance. The book that follows *Kitāb al-Jabr wa 'l-Muqābala* (The Book of Completion and Balancing) is the *Kitāb al-Waçāyā* (The Book of Testaments), a practical application of the algebraic equations to cases of inheritance.[34] According to al-Khwārizmī himself, certain jurists used algebraic calculations to solve their problems. After the invention of algebra, this discipline would become inextricably linked to the calculation of inheritances and bequests, the *Hisāb al-farā'iz* (Calculation of Obligations).

By founding a science on the calculation of unknowns (called *ash-Shay'* or "the Thing," the term also used to designate the deity enveloped in the unknown), independently of what they represent, and to do so submitting to the rules of demonstration, al-Khwārizmī invented a brand-new discipline that had emerged neither among the Greeks (Euclid, Heron, Diophantine) nor the Indians (Aryabhata, Brahmagupta), whose works were already circulating in Arabic-language milieus.

Starting with this invention and the dense body of work that moved it forward and allowed it to flourish in Arabic, the field of influence exerted by Arab mathematics in the medieval West began to spread, whether in arithmetic, algebra, or geometry. Twelfth-century Europe rediscovered Euclid following the Latin translation of the *Elements* based on Arabic adaptations. Many other Latin translations out of Arabic would change hands among learned circles of Europe. It is now a known fact that the most inventive European mathematician of the thirteenth century, Fibonacci, knew Arabic and traveled widely on scientific missions to gain knowledge at the source.[35]

But the Arab contribution to mathematics cannot be reduced to the limited circulation it experienced during the Middle Ages. The traditional opposition between medieval and modern science does not stand up to scrutiny. Two scientists separated in time by several centuries can be "contemporaries" by virtue of their research: this is the case of Fārisī (thirteenth-century algebraist) and Descartes (seventeenth century) for number theory; or the work of al-Karajī (eleventh century) that applies arithmetic to algebra through operations called "polynomials" which, until the eighteenth century, formed the core of any treatise on algebra; or "Newton's binomial" and the table of coefficients called "Pascal's Triangle," which could already be found in the treatise of as-Samaw'al (twelfth century).[36]

As we follow the footsteps of the mathematicians that pursued the path opened by al-Khwārizmī (for whom algebra is conceived as a science meant to resolve both numerical and geometrical problems), we discover that the articulation of algebra and geometry created a very active and creative school of thought. Sharaf al-Dīn al-Tūsī (late twelfth c.) is a brilliant illustration. This mathematician notably intuited what is called "Newton's Polygon."[37] His oeuvre includes several innovations that only Descartes and Fermat would later surpass. His elaborate numerical methods leave the work of Viète far behind.

By including the contributions of Arab mathematics in a common history, we realize that the usual classifications are overturned. This can be illustrated by the history of parallels, from Euclid to Henri Poincaré, registering along the way pertinent remarks by Arab mathematicians from the Middle Ages, a period which, if only for that reason, must not be considered a dark age. For during that time, sovereign, nonconstrained reason was pondering theoretical mathematics and, via experimentation, could put it into practice. And this spirit endured until the seventeenth century in Europe, when another break took place.

It is noteworthy that mathematics expressed in Arabic was already becoming international, an attribute normally associated with modern, Western science. In the end, mathematics is neither Arab, Western, nor European; but there was a language that, for a time, had the privilege of serving as the vehicle for research carried out by subjects belonging to diverse ethnicities, nations, and beliefs. Beyond difference, and by virtue of an array of syntheses, the history of mathematics is one and undivided: it had its time in Greek, Arabic, Latin, and finally in the modern languages of Europe.

If the example of mathematics radicalizes the use of civilization in the singular, we shall see that the opposing viewpoint actually reinforces this use as well. Suppose that we shift from science to something more mystical, that we migrate from an objective discourse to subjective expression, that we listen to the voice of inner experience rather than the testimony of reason; we shall see that, despite differences in belief, the notion of a common diachrony is plausible, even beyond the typical pattern of convergences shared by all mystics that transcend particular rites.

Here once again, Sufism is the heir to various speculative and spiritual traditions. Based on Koranic meditation, Sufism has joined with Neoplatonist interpretations, monastic disciplines, desert Anchorites, Zoroastrian enlightenment values, the ascetic retreat of the Brahmans, or even the paradoxical thought of Taoism, based on the union of opposites, the tension between masculine and feminine and the time of permanent creation. Sufism is thus a spirituality that draws on the thinking and experience of earlier traditions, having matured by listening to and assimilating numerous schools and methods, some of which had already made productive encounters among themselves, while others had never made contact.

It is this intermingling that results in the depth of religious feeling that characterizes Sufism, which René Guénon believes to be the most complete in the way it accounts for what he calls "the single doctrine," whose truth he has perceived throughout his peregrinations among the great spiritual traditions. Indeed, consistent with his conclusions, he himself entered into Islam by way of Sufism, which led to a gathering of disciples around the journal *Etudes traditionnelles*, a breeding ground of intellectual converts in Europe, including Martin Lings and Michel Chodkiewicz, two of the better known.

As in other areas, this encompassing capacity is a gift of Islamic expansion, one that fulfills the Koranic promise to promote Islam as a median nation ("And thus we have made you a community of the middle way," Koran 2:143). It is in this respect that Toynbee identified the singularity of Islam, the only entity to have come into simultaneous contact with the borders of Western Europe, Byzantium, China, India, and sub-Saharan Africa. This contiguousness in diversity afforded Arabic the privilege of coming into contact with areas covered by Latin, Greek, and Chinese, with Sanskrit added to the integrated areas that made available all the knowledge written down in Persian, Syriac, Aramaic, Hebrew, Demotic, and Amharic. Islam bound together these disparate traditions, uniting and reviving them, one after the other.

This was the situation that allowed the "greatest Sufi master," Ibn 'Arabī (Murcia 1165–Damascus 1240) such diverse associations. His oeuvre is so multiform and open-ended that people have considered him at times an "unconscious Christian" (the Spanish Jesuit Miguel Asín Palacios[38]) and at others, a Neoplatonist (the Egyptian A. E. Affifi,[39] a student of Reynold A. Nicholson). While preserving their originality, complexity, and polyphony, Henry Corbin inflected his works, and rightly so, with certain Gnostic traditions, which move him closer to a Shiite or Iranian sensibility.[40] Or again, the Japanese scholar Toshihiko Izutsu reads him in surprisingly enriching proximity with Taoism.[41] This plurality of interpretations led Michel Chodkiewicz to remind us that Ibn 'Arabī was first of all a devout, orthodox Sunni, beyond all his inventiveness and the discrepancies caused by the tension between law and experience. This tension exists in all mystical practice but reaches its high point with Ibn 'Arabī.

Remaining within the Western sphere alone, it is still possible to trace the evolution of mysticism over time and place. Without forcing things too much, I invite the reader to take the example of experience with the invisible. The first link in our chain will be Plotinus, when he speaks in theological terms of the *aphatos* (the ineffable). I would then add Philo of Alexandria, even though he was active two centuries before Plotinus. For the latter continued the Greek tradition exclusively (mid–third century), while Philo (in the early first century) opened the way, for all descendants of monotheism, to an articulation between Hellenistic philosophy and revealed Scriptures.

Philo, a Greek-speaking Jew, meditated upon the face of the invisible by associating Greek concepts with the Bible. He read the word of Yahweh addressed to Moses: "Thou canst not see my face" (Exodus 33:20) by invoking the *aperinoutos* (the inconceivable), the *aperigraptos* (uncircumscribable), and the *atheatos* (impossible to contemplate). Thus, when Moses ascended into the cloud, he would "understand that God, in his act of existing, is incomprehensible to all creatures, and see that he is, in actual fact, invisible."[42]

Thus is the subject placed in the presence of mystery, and language will then face the challenge of somehow representing the unspeakable and the invisible. This place opened up for the

"Wholly Other Here-Now" was massively occupied by the
Church Fathers, and it will be one of them who will constitute
my third link in the chain, since Philo's direct descendants were
Christian only. Among the Fathers, two voices emerge together
that meditated on the same Old Testament verse. John Chrysostom (344–407) equates vision and knowledge: "For incorporeal
virtues have neither eye nor eyelid, and what is for us vision is
for them knowledge. Thus, whenever you should hear 'No one
has ever seen God,' know that you have heard that no one has
ever known God in his essence with full exactness."[43]

But Gregory of Nyssa (second half of the fourth c.), though
he was cognizant of the conversion of vision into knowledge,
persisted in his quest of boundlessness involving the eye. Since
that which one is seeking to see has no specific shape, the quest
becomes infinite, involving every minute of every day, and is
equated with an aesthetic quest, the search for Beauty, or the
lover's quest, that of unfulfilled desire: "No limit can interrupt
the momentum of the ascent to God, since, on the one hand,
Beauty knows no bounds, and on the other, there can be no
satisfying the ever greater desire felt toward Him."[44]

Yet there is a verse in the Koran that is the exact equivalent of
the biblical verse, regarding the same Moses-related episode. It
is almost a direct quote, but re-created in the spirit of the bor-
rowing language: *Lan tarānī* ("Thou shall see me not"; Koran
7:143). The formula in Arabic is so striking by the force of its
concision that it has been transformed into a station where the
journeying Sufi makes a stop, and this is my fourth link in the
chain, illustrated by the written commentary of one of the masters of the Path, Qushayri (986–1072) in his *tafsīr* (Koranic
exegesis).[45]

In the Sufi's commentary, as it happens, one can glimpse the
outlines of the two fourth-century Fathers' perspective. First,
Moses is represented as a lover drunk with desire, as he submits
his request to God: "My Lord, show me Thyself, that I may
look at You" (Koran 7:413). His mind was so muddled that he
did not realize the senselessness of his request, for the lover

knows that the face of the loved one is so ever-present to him that he would not recognize it, were it to actually appear before him. What, then, of the object of love that cannot even be figured at all? It is only once he had returned to a state of sobriety that Moses grasped the impossibility of his request, which had confused vision and knowledge. Yet this confusion is but the sign of the infinite quest of a desire that nothing can fulfill. And Moses would be vindicated with God's choosing of him as one of his closest, as Qushayri would state, finally, in his commentary on the remainder of the Koranic episode, granting Moses the privilege of hearing the inaudible, thereby situating him via the sense of hearing in closest proximity with the "Wholly Other Here-Now." This privilege would give Moses the power to "hear the scraping of the *qalam* on the Tablet" when God was dictating his commandments to the angel-scribes to complete the Decalogue.

Asín Palacios is quick to enumerate the similarities and overlaps between Ibn 'Arabī on the one hand, and on the other John of the Cross and Theresa of Avila, while emphasizing Ibn 'Arabī's highly accurate reprise of Plotinus.[46] He also points to numerous overlaps between the sheikh and the Fathers. By virtue of his grounding in Neoplatonist fundamentals (where the historian perceives him as two centuries ahead of European Renaissance thinkers), and his commonality with the Church Fathers' observations, we can legitimately include Ibn 'Arabī as the fifth link in the chain. This brings us to the final link of our diachronic timeline, represented by two great mystics of the Catholic Counter-Reformation, as expressed in the Castilian language.

There are sufficient grounds for associating these links with our example of the experience of vision, which in this case is nothing other than intuitive knowledge.[47] Thus, Ibn 'Arabī and John of the Cross concur on the issue of excluding from contemplation anything that is not God. Both have an agnostic concept of a God inaccessible to anyone that is not Him. Contemplation reaches perfection whenever it casts off any analogy with Creation. It is bounded by the metaphysical experience of a featureless God, obscure, shrouded in mystery, awe-inspiring. The mystic advances toward Him, his mind a blank, full of spiritual woe, which is thought to be the key to contemplation. Both Ibn 'Arabī and John of the Cross share the features of this quest for a God who "has neither form nor face." And memory "goes forth assuredly, devoid of form and of face, closer in likeness to God; for the more it clings to imagination, the further from God it wanders . . . , because God . . . does not fall into imagination."[48] Thus speaks John of the Cross in his commentary on line 3 of *Llama de amor viva* (Bright Fire of Love). The same words might have served Ibn 'Arabī to comment on one of the lines of his *Interpreter of Desires*.[49]

What I have presented here in three different areas is far from exhaustive, to be taken as guidelines only. Our civilizing structure is based, in its very difference, upon identical scenes and trajectories. Literature provides a perfect illustration, with the extraordinary resonance between Dante and Ibn 'Arabī,[50] as does the intersection between Romanesque and Arab traditions with regard to both the themes and prosody of courtly love.[51] Or again, the circulation of the literary myth of love that drives one to madness and death, a myth unknown to the Greeks and Latins, or to the Hindus and Chinese, one invented by the Arabs during the latter half of the seventh century with the legend of Majnūn and Layla. This myth would migrate to Europe to be embodied in Tristan and Isolde, Romeo and Juliet, and would be revived again by the figure of the young Werther. The theme experienced more recent incarnations among the surrealists, with Breton's *Amour fou* and Aragon's *Fou d'Elsa*.[52] Another crossing over involves the effect in the West of the *Thousand and One Nights*, from Galland to Borges and Michel Butor, and along the way, Potocki, Beckford, Restif de la Bretonne, Eugène Sue, Alexandre Dumas, and Proust,[53] not to forget numerous filmmakers fascinated by this myth, from Pasolini to Raoul Ruiz.[54]

This same civilizing structure can be tested in philosophy (notably the role of Averroes and his Latin and Hebrew descendants, with regard to the notion of separation that would eventually lead to the theory of secularism[55]) as well as in political thought (particularly with the adaptation by Fārābī into Islam of Plato's utopian city[56]) or in theology (where we note how Islam, before advocating "orthopraxis," contained everything necessary to metaphysical questioning, the same encountered by Christianity[57]).

The enrichment of these various fields is owed essentially to the special relationship between Arabic and Greek. Like the myth, which functioned poetically and philosophically from Hölderlin to Heidegger, according to which the German language was heir to Greek and thereby founded the European Ur (Greek being embodied in the German vehicle), a similar fiction was projected onto Arabic. A witness to this is the Jewish poet from Grenada, Moshe IbnEzra (around 1060–1135), one of the three great Hebrew poetic voices of Andalusia (along with Ibn Gabirol and Yehuda Halevi)—IbnEzra, a fluent speaker, writer, and thinker in Arabic, was so competent that he was able to claim that "Arabic among languages is like Spring among the seasons."[58] It is true that among Arabic speakers, poetry seems innate (*tabʿ*), whereas it must be acquired by other language groups (*tatabbuʿ*).[59] In addition, though, historical circumstance has stored in Arabic all the meanings accumulated in Greek, as Rāzī praised in the tenth century: He notes the proper care (*al-iʿtinā aç-çahīha*) displayed by this language to promote wisdom, philosophy, mathematics, logic, politics, physics, and metaphysics.[60] It is thanks to his ability to read the Greeks in Arabic translation that IbnEzra, in his poetic and ethical quest, becomes familiar with Hermes, Pythagoras, Galen, Hippocrates, Ptolemy, Diogenes, Socrates, Plato, and Aristotle, all of whom he cites abundantly along with Arab thinkers of Hellenist inspiration (Jāhiz, Kindī, Thābit ibn Qurra, Fārābī, Rāzī, and the Ikhwān aç-Çafā), as well as the Koran or the

Bible (quoted in both Hebrew and Arabic in the same codex),[61] or various masters of the rabbinical tradition.[62]

At the other end of the Islamic world, in central Asia, somewhat earlier, and this time in the fields of science and philosophy, al-Bīrūnī, born in the Khwārizm in 973 and thought to have died in Ghazna around 1050, testifies to the same solidarity between Arabic and Greek. A Persian speaker with knowledge of Sanskrit, a writer of Arabic, this author knew everything about astronomy that was knowable at that time among the Greek, Hindu, and Arabic legacies. He undertook a masterful synthesis of this science, with additional consideration of the Chinese input with regard to chronological bases. He was the first to test the hypothesis of the Earth's rotation on its own axis to explain diurnal movement. But he failed to draw the ultimate conclusions, figuring that this consideration would not change his calculations regarding the establishment of astronomical tables that located the positions of the heavenly bodies.[63]

During his research trip in India (around 1038), he communicated with his subcontinental counterparts as a representative of Hellenism. He was struck by the analogy between contemporary India and ancient Greece, due to the cohabitation of pagan mythology and rational thought. He was annoyed, however, by India's ethnocentrism and its ignorance of the Greeks. Whenever he would present to his peers a solution issuing from Greek knowledge and developed by Arabs, his Indian counterparts, impressed, would inquire as to which Indian master had provided him with this pertinent answer. He also observed that India had not produced a Socrates who knew how to distinguish between *logos* and *muthos*, at the risk of defying the law of the city and putting his life in jeopardy.[64] Thus, al-Bīrūnī discussed with Indian pundits and sages in the name of Greek philosophical and scientific discourse as decanted into Arabic.

Al-Bīrūnī's attraction to Hellenism was such that he was one of the few to propose a Greek etymology for the word "Sufism," which designates, as we know, mystic experience in Islam. He derives it, in fact, from the Greek *sophia*, since Sufis are sages (*al-hukamā*).[65] According to al-Birūnī, theoreticians of Sufism were mistaken when they derived the word from the Arabic *çoffa*,[66] the bench on the veranda that extended the house of the Prophet in Medina, where the homeless poor would gather. Future sages would make the connection between these beggars, who they assumed to have chosen this austere life and its vow of poverty, and to have thereby founded the order of the Sufis. Among other conventional etymologies—*çafa*, purity; *çafwa*, elite; *çaff*, first-ranked in spiritual hierarchy—al-Birūnī refuted the most common of all, that of *çūf*, wool, with reference to the woolen habit worn by the seeker.[67]

This link between Greek and Arabic was not merely an operative fiction that worked efficiently for the growth of science, philosophy, mysticism, and poetry. It also constituted a historical reality that enabled a finer philological approach that comes to light when one observes how much Greek has been deposited into the Arabic language. For the Greek in Arabic can participate in the history of the Greek text itself, when the Arabic translation testifies to a state more remote in time than the oldest manuscript to have been handed down in Greek. Roselyne Dupont-Roc and Jean Lallot mention this in passing in the introduction to their translation of *Poetics*, observing that the Arabic version testifies to an older state of the Greek text, capable of playing a precious role in establishing the Aristotelian text.[68] But what was merely a praiseworthy intention, if not wishful thinking, becomes fully operational with Marwan Rashed: As he shows in his edition of the text *Of Generation and Corruption*, "the Arabic translation from the latter half of the 9th century, heretofore unexploited by the editors of the *GC*, casts considerable light on the text and its history. This translation, undoubtedly done by Içhāq ibn Hunayn (died in 910), like its Syriac model ascribed to Hunayn ibn Içhāq (died in 873), is lost in the original language, but was reconstituted with the help of its Latin version done by Gerard of Cremona in the 12th century and its Hebrew version done by Zerahyiah ibn Içhāq in the 13th century."[69] The relation of Greek to Arabic can thus be considered heuristic. In fact, we can say with some assurance that, in the end, it would be hard to call oneself a Hellenist without a thorough knowledge of Arabic.

Historically and philologically, then, Arabic became central to the network of knowledge woven among Greek, Syriac, Latin, and Hebrew, which would in turn help to open up the Arab and Islamic reference and grant it the place it had rightfully earned as a participant in the common *arche*, or source, at work in the founding of Western civilization.

These are the issues that should contribute to clearing up misperceptions in the West as to the Arab contribution, and also recover for Muslims a repressed aspect of their past. A rigorous exercise in the recovery of this memory would prove liberating by forcing Muslims to recognize their intrinsic Westernness. This would be a prerequisite for Islam to get back in step with civilization, the very one that Islam helped pass on to the West. This realization was already being felt in the nineteenth century. It was implicitly at work in the writings of Muhammad 'Abduh, whose project involved modernizing Islam by bringing it back into more fruitful contact with the West. The same plan was more explicitly laid out by Taha Hussein during the 1920s and '30s. Today, however, the trend is heading in the other direction, toward an exclusivist Islamization of modernity. The call to Muslims to assume their historic Western roots has fallen on deaf ears, at the very moment when the world is moving into a post-Western era, into which we Muslims might have entered more proudly, not quite so powerless if we had already Westernized. What a waste of time and resources! Such a missed opportunity! We are so out of touch!

Earlier in this text, I stated that, to preserve the complexity of Islam, we need to approach it as a civilization, a religion, and a political aspiration. The example just developed, concerning Sufism, provides insight into the religious question through the poetic intensity and metaphysical fervor of the inner experience, which is capable of surpassing the institutional edifices of belief. What matters most in this experience is perhaps the energy it elicits, the crucial questioning it provokes. Since it asks more questions than it answers, it attracts modern thinkers and adapts easily to new situations. Such names as Hölderlin, Nietzsche, and Georges Bataille evoke a craving for the mystic, and the mere mention of anything mystic puts rationalist or secular reduction on hold.

I now think about religion as a system of belief that provides something absolute that will help in a person's self-formation, at the imaginary and symbolic levels, in order to better deal with reality. It is a psychic and ethical prerequisite that leads a person to take charge of himself or herself as a subject capable of assuming the status of citizen. This is still the case in societies and milieus that continue to hold strong religious beliefs. Hence, Islam continues to play a preeminent role in the world, since it is still incumbent upon that religion to produce men and women meant to renew the social pact.

Yet danger lurks whenever we approach Islam as a totality, and not as three separate factors, for it is the totalizing vision that is fatal to civilization. And this is precisely what is taking place today: Through their misunderstanding of how potentially effective each of these three factors can be—civilization, religion, and politics—Muslims are unwittingly forgetting or negating their own tradition. They are reducing that tradition to a set of received notions that predispose them to receiving the message preached by fundamentalist militants. This amnesia-inducing confusion has produced the barbaric contemporary moment in which we currently find ourselves.

If barbarity is the negation of civilization, it might be said that Islam has always lived under this threat from within, one that has nevertheless always been contained whenever political authorities realized that, beyond their own survival, their first duty was to protect the edifice of civilization from those whose project aimed at its destruction. Civilization, we now know, is the product of mixtures, not totalities. As soon as a voice emerges to claim purity of origin and scripture, as soon as energy is spent on identifying what it is that is disturbing this presumed purity, inquisitors begin drawing up lists of outside intruders that have muddied the clear waters of the fundaments. This search for wholeness has regularly found adherents within Islam.

The first to have compiled the complete catalog of disruptive elements is probably the late thirteenth-century theologian Ibn Taymiyyah, considered today by Wahhabis and fundamentalists as their founding father. In his zeal to purify Islam, he turned nihilist, negating civilizing elements for the sake of religious rules, thereby ridding the religion of all those elements that had acclimatized Islam to so many cultures that it shared, and that had kept at bay the temptation to turn inward on itself. Among the timber to be felled in the "forest of Islam,"[70] Ibn Taymiyyah points to areas where philosophy originated (Greek seeds), where Sufism thrived (grafts involving Indian, Iranian, and Christian essences), where the cult of saints evolved (rooted in the pagan humus of Mesopotamia, Greece, and Egypt), and where a too-biblical interpretation of the Koran prevailed (one that introduced what theologians of a more enlightened age had called the *isrā'iliyyāt*, a term that implies a return to the biblical and rabbinical corpus so as to give substance to Koranic allusions and ellipses).[71] Oddly enough, in his lengthy negative catalog, not a word is said about science and technology, whose foreign origin is glaringly obvious.

One cannot help but notice a similarity here with today's fundamentalists, who make shrewd use of technology, in their eyes the only Western value worth conserving. In doing so, they provide a perfect illustration of nihilism taken to its extremes, as defined by Leo Strauss.[72] According to Strauss, nihilism first expresses itself through a negation of modern civilization based on citizenship and democracy. This negative assessment of modernity comes down to a more general anti-Western sentiment whose first appearance within Islam is easily datable: It emerged with the foundation of the Muslim Brotherhood in Egypt at the end of the 1920s. This corresponds, rather astonishingly, to the European nihilism that Leo Strauss was critiquing, and its objects of hatred are the same (see Oswald Spengler and Carl Schmitt[73]), a "hyena's prophecy" of a similar sort,[74] whose target is the very foundation of Western modernity: liberalism, democracy, and parliamentarianism.

This anti-Western sentiment has made a comeback in the lands of Islam. As of the mid–nineteenth century, the first generations of reformist theologians were coming to the realization that they had lost their grip on civilization, and they attempted to reclaim it by seeking to assimilate and emulate the civilization that had laid claim to it, that is, the European civilization on the opposite shore. They needed to mesh the sources of Islam with the Western model they so admired. They had to fight against both local despotism and colonial hegemony, in the name of democratic and parliamentary principles. Their rallying cry, devoid of any nihilist tendencies, was to modernize Islam.

With the third generation of Muslim Brothers, the group's motives took a more radical turn: It was now a matter of Islamizing modernity. What does this mean? It requires that Islam retain nothing of Western modernity except its technology. Any claim to science would require rigors difficult to measure up to. For the rest, the movement's trailblazers wished to subject society to a total Islam, whereby civilization would decline, in favor of a politico-religious practice and an aggressive proselytizing aimed at conquering the world. At first a minority movement, the program eventually gained ground that had been ceded through a series of shortcomings and political failures, which I mentioned in chapter 3.

What happened next was the logical extension of triumphant nihilism, according to Leo Strauss's definition, when civilization itself becomes the target of destruction. For this reason, fundamentalism is not only a danger for world stability, it constitutes a threat to Islam itself. The primacy of politics is destroying Islam as both religion and civilization. The inhumanity of political demands made in the name of God is producing monsters, and these demands are undermining religion's humanizing role. To reduce belief to the single criterion of divine law is to stifle creative energy. We now face the challenge of inventing hospitable spaces for acts of transgression if we are to preserve our contact with the *arche* of Islam, entrusted to us to safeguard for its own sake and for what its actualizations will mean for generations to come.

This is our duty, to prevail over the new barbarians in a relentless struggle against those bent upon bringing down civilization. A further duty involves preserving the memory of what Islam contributed to this civilization. The war against this barbarity can be legitimized only through such an acknowledgment. Once the impressive, centuries-old accumulation of works produced by and about Islam is made manifest, it will become clear that such an acknowledgment is already underway in a substantial number of works produced, for instance, in French.[75]

If war should break out, it will be a civil war, and not one between Islam and the West, as the fundamentalists would have it. The famous phrase of Themistocles, "Strike if you will, but listen," requires that both sides be simultaneously in a state of war and of mutual recognition. This is how the world is built, our common destiny. For better or for worse, henceforward "the West and the East / can no longer remain apart."[76] But have they ever really been, in fact? Everything I have summarized in this and earlier chapters would prove the contrary.

I would like to close this chapter with two remarks. The first involves a fresh break with what is often perceived as an enigma, and the second amounts to a profession of faith that flows logically from the thesis I am attempting to illustrate.

Many observers find it astonishing that such a brilliant civilization could experience such an abrupt and definitive interruption. In my book *The Malady of Islam*,[77] I list a certain number of reasons that historians point to when explaining this phenomenon. I also emphasize that, no matter how pertinent such causes may be, the whole issue remains something of an enigma: a matter of divine intervention (Bossuet) or of the unconscious in history (Braudel). But the facts are there: During a five-century period (750–1250), Islam brought civilization to heights previously unknown, that would live on for five more, drawing on that first five centuries' capital until the early nineteenth century, when it came to the realization that civilization had moved on and settled elsewhere. *What went wrong?* This is the question each of us is asking, along with Bernard Lewis, who in this case fails to provide the kinds of answers we will need to overcome the crisis that is corrupting the civilizing principle.[78]

To this same question, I would propose an answer suggested by a great Arab mind of the ninth century, al-Jāhiz, a polygraph rationalist influenced by Hellenism, master of irony, in the manner of Voltaire. His pages devoted to Manichaeism are of special interest here. This belief, still very much alive at the time and embraced by minds of great distinction, was destined to die out, for, according to al-Jāhiz, the literature of its followers offered nothing stimulating or compelling. It contained no edifying maxims, or words of wisdom, no philosophy or sophisticated dialectics, no practical commentary on arts and crafts or useful political considerations. Al-Jāhiz, on the other hand, judged any book as inept unless it addressed matters of survival in the here and now, unless it defended its belief system by rational means. Any sensible person would turn away from a belief that asked nothing of its followers but blind faith.[79] We can extend the point al-Jāhiz is making, and state that when the symbolic and the imaginary are reduced to an absurd mythology composed of frivolous fables, we are faced with the defeat of reason and, consequently, with the end of sovereignty. In Baghdad when al-Jāhiz was writing, even sailors would "seek reason in things," and knew, for instance, that the tides were caused by the attraction of the moon, and not by "the breathing of a sea monster," as affirmed by Manichaean mythology.[80]

Not surprisingly then, among scholars working to advance the sciences at that time, documents provide no evidence of a single Manichaean. And yet the Manichaeism contemporary with al-Jāhiz "claimed to be not only a definitive religion impervious to any evolution, but also and especially an absolute science, a universal, encyclopedic culture that included all branches of knowledge."[81]

Islam in its period of decadence found itself in exactly the same situation as Manichaeism, as criticized by one of Islam's great civilizing minds: a definitively congealed belief system, abhorring any innovation; a conservative body of thought that shut out critical reasoning; an absence of scientists and scientific method. The arguments provided by Islam in its period of enlightenment are therefore the ones I use to castigate the Islam of darkness to which we are the rebellious heirs. Must we recall the earth's circling of the sun in order to remain cognizant that the momentum of decline ends in extinction?

In the *Dialogue of a Philosopher with a Jew and a Christian*, Abelard (the reinventor of the copula[82]) suggests that the character of the philosopher is identifiable as a Muslim, necessarily using Arabic, which our logician abbot perceives as the language of reason, the one a person ought to master if he wishes to broaden the field of possibilities that exercises of the intellect bring to light, to grasp the relation between words and things. This is why Abelard praises Arabic and encourages those close to him to familiarize themselves with it. Thus, at a time when Arabic was the vehicle of civilization, it was not unthinkable to imagine Abelard urging his fellow Christians to "Arabize." And now that civilization is Western, I will in turn urge those whose origin I share to "Westernize."

An advancement of civilization, whichever one it might be, no longer belongs only to its inventors. It must become the property of any human being who wishes to acquire it. Once assimilated, it is not destined to remain as it was upon reception. All innovations must necessarily adapt to their new circumstances. Hence, the Westernization of a non-Westerner is not doomed to reproduce the West, but to improve it and contribute to moving beyond its current boundaries, engaging that path of infinite perfectibility linked to the very notion of civilization, with all its shifts and migrations. The Westernized subject will watch these moves with the vigilance of those who believe more in the flow of the quest than in the fixity of truths and values already acquired.

# CHAPTER 5

# Enlightenment between High and Low Voltage

Two distinct periods in Islamic history can be described as doubly infused with an Enlightenment spirit: the early participation in the surge of civilization from the ninth century onward, and the desire to join the civilizing movements of the nineteenth century. Upstream, so to speak, as early as the mid–eighth century, Islam was establishing the beginnings, and downstream, during the nineteenth century, it was experiencing the effects and attempting to adapt, without ever really succeeding.

Between 750 and 1050, authors were giving evidence of an astonishing freedom of thought in their approach to religions and the phenomenon of belief. This is the point I would like to emphasize, since Enlightenment values have always taken aim at the dogmatism, fanaticism, and superstition that religious beliefs convey. And it was just this sort of critique that was being developed among scholars and thinkers in the lands of Islam during the period labeled as the Dark Ages of the European Middle Ages.

These scholars and thinkers subjected their analyses to the test of reason, honoring one of the basic principles of the Enlightenment. This phenomenon took place at a moment of great intellectual excitement and intense exchange, a little more than a century after the advent of Islam, at a time when its followers were seeking to establish a tradition capable of measuring up to much more sophisticated systems of thought. It was also a moment when newcomers to Islam still had in mind the theological principles that made up the edifice of the beliefs of their birth and education (Judaism, various Christian sects, Manichaeism, or Zoroastrianism).

Ibn al-Muqaffaʿ (720–56) is the first of these thinkers, some of whose most salient notions I now present. Iranian by birth, still steeped in Zoroastrian and Manichaean traditions, he was one of the earliest to compose Arabic prose, most notably with *Kalila wa Dimna*,[1] where he adapted into Arabic a Pahlavi version of Indian fables that date back to the *Panchatantra* and the *Tantrakhyayika*. In his introduction to this collection, Ibn al-Muquaffaʿ criticizes religions and praises reason. In his view, morality is independent from belief and what is *mulhid* can be virtuous.[2] He held that, despite their great variety and mutual disagreements, all denominations include three kinds of followers: those who inherit their faith from their father, those who are forced to adopt a religion, and those who join a temporally powerful religion in order to fulfill their worldly ambitions. Furthermore, Ibn al-Muqaffaʿ observes that few people are capable of justifying their belief. Following this critique, however, our author retreats somewhat and accepts a common basis on which all beliefs agree, which comes down to moral principles that, though positive in themselves, are expressed negatively, as prohibitions (thou shalt not kill, lie, bear false witness, deceive, steal, etc.), stipulations that herald the ethical strategy of an Enlightenment philosopher such as Kant with his "postulates of practical reason."[3]

In another work, *Epistle on Friendship*, Ibn al-Muqaffaʿ addresses the caliph on politics. He suggests that clerics must answer to the prince, and that lawmaking be removed from the realm of religion and placed under political control. Since it is impossible to do away with religion altogether, better that it be overseen by the prince. Several orientalists, including Goitein and Gabrieli, have concluded that if Ibn al-Muqaffa's suggestion had been acted upon, Islam might have experienced an early secularization and avoided the doctrinal pitfalls that endure to this day.

With Ibn al-Muqaffa', we come up against the whole Western issue of double authority, the prince and the pontiff. Addressing this very duality would constitute the grand philosophical design that led the West toward Enlightenment through a series of stages, among them Dante's *On Monarchy* (1304), Machiavelli's *Discourses* (1513–20), Jean Bodin's *Six Books of the Republic* (1576), and Spinoza's *Tractatus Theologico-Politicus* (1670), as well as Hobbes's *Leviathan* (1651). However different their contexts, issues, and aims, all these thinkers, in the wake of Ibn al-Muqaffa', question the hierarchy of the two powers: either they call for the autonomy of the temporal and the spiritual, or they subject the latter to the former. The current scope of Ibn al-Muqaffa's proposals should not be reduced by associating them with power as it was exercised in the Persian Empire, where religion and royalty were concentrated in a single person.

Ibn al-Muqaffa' also undertakes a radical critique of the Koran, fragments of which have come down to us via a ninth-century author's refutation of it. To begin with, he cites numerous examples from the Koran that neither reason nor intuition can conceive. He then declares that the anthropomorphisms applied to God contradict his invisibility and mystery. He calls the prophets impostors, citing as an example the founder of Islam's overzealous campaign to conquer a worldly realm. And last, he develops a critique of monotheism in general, which he says cannot escape dualism, due to the question of evil and its presence in the world and within Man himself.

Later on, in early ninth-century Baghdad, there emerged the *mu'tazila*, those theologians whose thought was nourished by reason. By equating God with transcendence alone, they withdraw him from the world, in a sense, and return the earthly sojourn to the responsibility of man, who will face evil with his free will. But this movement gradually moved away from the spirit of the Enlightenment as it drew closer to the caliph, and out of its doctrine arose an ideology that the coercive state enforced through constraint and violence, starting with an inquisition initiative undertaken in 883 by the caliph al-Ma'mūn, whose aim was to pursue his opponents and convert them.[4]

Yet there was still scope for discussion and exchange at this time among various beliefs. Among the great minds of the period, let us mention the Christian Hunayn Ibn Içhāq (803–73), who played a major role in transmitting the Greek scientific and philosophical corpus. This multidisciplinary thinker, a polyglot at ease in three cultures (Syriac, Greek, Arab) and acquainted with two others (Persian and Indian), resembles the great figures of the European Renaissance, and was once compared to Erasmus. In one of his books, he transcends his own faith and, freed from any apologetics or polemics, makes use of pure logic to understand first how truth might be apprehended by religions, and second how error creeps in and prevails as truth among believers.

Another of these "free thinkers" is al-Warrāq (died around 861),[5] who criticized his own religion (Islam) and all other religions by pointing out their contradictions and implausibility when examined through the prism of reason. In the end, he came up with a logical monotheism that oversteps established beliefs and requires from them no authentication. This critical approach to established religions situates its author in amazing proximity to Enlightenment deism.

Many other authors give evidence of such critical judgment, even tinged with skepticism. But it was undoubtedly Abū Bakr Rāzī (ca. 854–925) who appears the closest in spirit to the Enlightenment. He is the celebrated physician and philosopher known in the Latin world by the name Rhazes. In a discussion that opposes him to another Rāzī[6] and which relates one of the most radical controversies, one of the most divisive moments in

Islamic history, our philosopher doctor affirms that, in order to acquire knowledge, the divine gift of reason is sufficient. There is no need, he says, to believe in any particular revelation, as they only cause dissension, disputes, and wars. At best, prophets are imposters or lunatics. Ordinary people have no use for divine law. They can think on their own, inspired by their theoretical and practical intelligence. Rāzī asserts that the philosophy has nothing to gain by beliefs based upon superstition, legend, and mystification, overlaid with ignorance and dogmatism. He also criticizes the preoccupation with ritual, which creates an obsession with imaginary impurities. He considers himself more valuable than men of religion: As a physician and man of science, does he not render a greater service to humanity by relieving his fellow man of sickness and suffering?[7] He was someone who believed in positive progress, convinced that he had improved the knowledge passed down from Galen and that subsequent generations of scientists would in turn improve upon his own legacy. In other words, he believed that scientific knowledge is always temporary, in constant flux and continuous advancement.

We might well wonder why this sequence of critical thought was interrupted, why it was not relayed in such a way as to enter the common political vocabulary, why these early harbingers of the Renaissance and the Enlightenment never gave way to practical projects within Muslim societies, never transformed the collective imagination.

Not that the mingling of ideas had no ideological effects at all, or never affected any political events. Still, the theological controversy yielded only two paradigmatic types of political outcome: on the one hand, it served to legitimize a power shift toward one or another of the rival parties (as in early Islam, with the opposition between the Umayyads and the partisans of Ali, between Sunni and Shiite); and on the other, in an often-repeated move (analyzed by Ibn Khaldūn,[8] 1332–1406), a purifying reform project would be launched to restructure power according to whatever vision of prophetic origin one happened to espouse (as illustrated by the Almoravids and the Almohads in the eleventh and twelfth centuries in the Islam of the western Mediterranean). This would appear to be the historic structure of the link between thought and state, between ideology and power, between theology and politics.

Equally important historically is the defeat of the *mu'tazila* in the mid–ninth century, some forty years after their triumph. Their expulsion from the seat of power took place at the same radical level of inquisitorial violence that they themselves had exercised during the period of their hegemony. And their ideas, which could have been pivotal for the evolution of Islam, were defeated once and for all around the year 1000, after two centuries of resistance. There can be no doubt that their notion of a "created Koran" could have triggered a process that would relativize the sacred quality of the Law, rendering it less untouchable. Their notions of free will, choice, and human responsibility in the face of evil could have enabled Muslims to get accustomed to the key ideas of modernity—freedom and the individual—that were to vanish from their mental horizon.

What we see instead is an absence of the notion of freedom in the social and political sense, the nonemergence of the basics that eventually crystallized into the concept of the individual. The praise of reason, if not its triumph over dogma, did not pick up on the signs that heralded these future issues.

One feature that is worth recalling, since it is most likely behind the emergence of these enlightened forerunners, is the quality of tolerance, another Enlightenment value. Islam proved relatively amenable toward other monotheistic beliefs based on revelation (Jews, Christians, and the enigmatic Sabians who, as I have already mentioned, were identified as Neoplatonists, Zoroastrians, or even followers of the Buddha). This disposition, along with a few Koranic principles (such as the verse that says, "There shall be no compulsion in religion," Koran 2:256), encouraged the liberals in the cosmopolitan atmosphere of ninth–tenth-century Baghdad to speak out and organize gatherings

for the purpose of theological argumentation where members
of each sectarian group would express their point of view with
no fear of reprisal. The Manichaeans, for instance, were very
active in these gatherings. This kind of "disputation" and the
literary genre that emerged from it provide us with testimony
of the critical, rational approach to religion and the phenomenon of belief.

This Islamic "tolerance," however relative it may be, was
pointed out in the most famous essays to deal with this theme
in the age of Enlightenment: Both Voltaire and Locke perceive
here a lesser evil when faced with the irredentism of their contemporaries, which precludes any means of survival for the
minority sects that share evangelical beliefs with majority
groups.

Furthermore, during the first four centuries of the Hegira,
during its formative period, Islam was building itself as a religion, theology, culture, and civilization, with all the dynamic
force required of such a phase. This took place in the ferment of
exchange and adaptation to a multiplicity of previous traditions
with their own profuse legacies. This time of ingurgitation, assimilation, and enrichment required openness by definition. It
was around the fifth century Hegira (eleventh c.) that the trend
toward fixedness started to prevail. At this point, the establishing of the Koran was finished, and the text's definitive form
was adopted. From this point forward, all competing revisions
and variants would be banned, a decision that provoked bitter
debates, ones that today's historians are seeking to reconstitute
and put back on the table.

It was also at this time that the notion of innovation (*bid'a*)
was stamped with a paralyzing negativity, to the point where
orientalists, in order to translate the term, resort to a pejorative
adjective ("blameworthy innovation") when designating Muslim jurists' disapproval, even though these lawmakers had been
accustomed to thinking of it in a positive light. Indeed, the
notion was an essential one for legitimizing things new and
foreign that they encountered as they came in contact with

civilizations more complex than their own, with fields of knowledge more extensive than their experience in the comparatively archaic milieu of Medina, with its infinitely narrower frame of reference. The negative vision of *bid'a* wiped out the more positive face as soon as the political-religious authorities deemed sufficient what had already been elaborated. Thus, the effort of theological construction was replaced by the rigors of orthopraxis, strict oversight of ritual practices, and the standardization of worship, all communitarian reference points placed under the surveillance of social censorship.

In this situation of closure, vast works would be produced, synthesizing theology, mysticism, and philosophy, outlining a practical morality, a kind of guide to living that buttressed the primacy of religion. Such syntheses are by all appearances definitive, with the most eloquent expression still being the work of Abū Hāmid Ghazālī (1058–1111),[9] *Ihyā 'ulūm ad-Dīn* (The Revival of Religious Sciences), which is still read today as if it were capable of addressing issues faced by people in the twenty-first century. We can only conclude that Islam's scholars believed that their edifice, once completed, had attained an unequaled degree of perfection, and that the aim henceforward would be to shield it from the forces of change, to preserve it for all time. This would explain why this period produced such a profusion of encyclopedias and dictionaries in all fields of knowledge.

To sum up, it is easy to see that Islam, during this time, was thinking in terms of "the end of history" and was putting the concept into practice. When we see its devastating effects, we realize what a malignant concept it can be, and how wary we should be of its use.

But the worst was yet to come, in the late thirteenth century, with the Hanbali exegete Ibn Taymiyyah (died 1328). He was to radicalize even further the notion of *bid'a*, nefarious in his view, searching out instances of its presence even in the encyclopedias and dictionaries of the eleventh century, which already marked the early stages of closure. Ibn Taymiyyah was constantly on the lookout for what he considered as an intrusion into the original abode, denouncing the introduction of Jewish, Christian, Greek, Manichaean, Mazdean, and Hindu motifs into systems supposedly inspired by the Koran alone. He castigated the effects of Greek philosophy, of Christian and Hindu mysticism, of polytheist saint worship, of pagan tomb visitation, all of which he considered a disfigurement of the primal edifice. This author, sworn enemy of Enlightenment, both its premises and its effects on Islam, would commit to posterity the matrix from which all future fundamentalisms would draw.

After this first period of intellectual fervor and enlightenment, the fourteenth century ushered in a protracted period of lethargy that would remain shrouded in darkness until the early nineteenth century. This long night was to glimpse the promise of daylight with the spread of Enlightenment ideas introduced into the lands of Islam by Bonaparte's expedition to Egypt (1798), which set off a veritable shock wave throughout the slumbering Arab East. Until then, Islam considered itself, if not superior, then at least the equal of Europe when it came to military might and standard of living. And yet here they were suddenly bested by weaponry, material goods, technical know-how, and scientific approaches unknown to them. There was a desire to understand the reasons behind Europe's advancement, which forced Muslims to acknowledge their historic backwardness and established a balance of power that left them in the position of weakness and dependency.

Awakened to this reality, Muslim men of letters in various lands of Islam (Arab, Turkish, Persian, Asian) came in contact with Enlightenment notions. Travelers from these regions visited the capitals of Europe and transmitted their enthusiastic reactions to their countrymen and fellow Muslims. The elites of these countries were soon in thrall to all things Western, and a veritable wave of Occidentalism swept the region. This yearning for Europe was expressed in state policy, whether it be through the reform effort of the *tanzimat*, introduced in the Ottoman Empire by Sultans Mahmut II (1808–39) and Abdülmacid I (1839–61), or the push for modernization in Egypt led by Mehmet 'Ali (1805–49).[10]

The new Enlightenment issues were apprehended in connection to the analogies, if not the premises, that Islamic tradition could put forth. Thus, the deism and tolerance preached by the new Europe found resonance with Akbarism, which structured the Ottoman, Arab, and Persian elite. This metaphysical and moral theory derived from the texts of the Andalusian religious philosopher Ibn 'Arabī, who spread his concept of the unity of Being and, as we saw earlier, steered Islamic belief toward a form of immanent deism alongside religious relativism, which rendered the Koran all the more relative, going so far as to allow for all forms of belief, even the most pagan among them. A European woman of the Enlightenment age, Lady Mary Montagu, wife of the English ambassador to the Ottoman court, whom I also mentioned earlier, testifies to this influence on the Ottoman elite, who did not consider other religions out of bounds but rather worthy of interest, perfectly intelligible and compelling.

In addition, the proximity of this "deism" to the philosophy of Spinoza (source of Enlightenment deism as well as Romanticism[11]) helped a number of these Muslims to respond to the Masonic message and join certain lodges, as did Emir Abdelkader (1807–83), disciple of his medieval master Ibn 'Arabī, whose message he reinterpreted before joining the ranks of the Freemasons.

Moreover, faced with the challenge of adapting to European Enlightenment innovations, Muslim theologians restored the primacy of reason, as advocated by Muhammad 'Abduh (1848–1905), mufti of Egypt, who wrote that in a case of conflict between reason and tradition, it is up to reason to decide. They in turn resorted to the notion of innovation (*bid'a*) in order to restore their inclination toward positivity as conceived by an earlier generation of jurists who, with the expansion of the empire, felt the need to adapt to circumstances and to acclimate to a level of civilization more advanced than that of seventh-century

Medina, the site of their faith's origins.[12] Thanks to this trend, the Ottomans were able to adopt the constitutional principle.

This notion is also combined with that of *maslaha* adopted in the tenth century by the Maliki school of Islam in the western Mediterranean: *maslaha* adapts the idea of *utilitas publica*, taking the public good into account when applying the law, correcting rules whenever it is proven that the common interest requires it (echoing the *corrigere jus propter utilitatem publicam* supported by Roman law). In this traditional perspective, Zurqāni, a Cairene theologian, proclaimed in 1710 the need to take new measures whenever new conditions arise: "We cannot find it strange that laws should adapt to circumstances."[13]

Muhammad ʿAbduh and his disciples would turn to these positivist notions (*bidʿa*, *maslaha*) to acclimate to Enlightenment principles and carry out political actions on their behalf, against both local despots and the colonial predations of Europe. With regard to the latter, they pointed out a certain inconsistency between principle and action when it came to European policy abroad. This argument was invoked in 1834, only four years after France's expedition into Algiers, in the preface of the first French-language book to issue from the Maghreb, *Le Miroir*, where author Hamdan Khodja observes that the French, by invading Algeria, were violating the revolutionary principles of 1789 and were therefore demonstrating an inconsistency between theory and practice: On the one hand, in Africa, they brought down an already constituted nation, people, and state, while at the same time they defended peoples, nations, and states in Europe in the process of constitution (Greece, Poland, Belgium).[14] I have referred to this dishonor in action as "the test of universals" that "Western aporia" must eventually confront.[15]

There are three distinct phases that show the more or less directly causal effects of Enlightenment in the wake of Muhammad ʿAbduh. First, Qāçim Amīn dealt with the symptomatic issue of women in two pamphlets that appeared in 1898 and 1900, in which he demanded loud and clear the enfranchisement of women and their release from seclusion, calling for the institution of an integrated society with the participation of women in schooling and the production of knowledge. Modernization for women would require that they unveil to enjoy freedom and equality. Such demands can also be informed by a positive vision of the *bid'a* and the *maslaha*, the principles of public interest that correspond to an Islam freed from the letter of the law to recover its spirit, in order to rethink the notion of *common* that makes sense out of *community*.

Next, Sheikh Ali Abderraziq (1888–1966) published an essay in 1925 titled *Islam and the Foundations of Governance*.[16] The author demonstrates that the notion of an Islamic state has never existed. He concludes that the caliphate, at the height of its splendor, under both the Umayyad and Abbasid rule, did not produce a new form of government but rather adopted the imperial structures of Byzantium and Persia, which had proven their administrative and military effectiveness. Contemporary Muslims were thus to build their states by drawing inspiration from the best of what other nations had produced—in other words, by emulating examples based on Enlightenment values, inspired by Montesquieu, Rousseau, Kant. Abderraziq also emphasizes that what matters most in the prophet Muhammad's experience is not his military or regal example but his spiritual and moral guidance. For him, Islam is a divine message and not a system of governance, a religion and not a state. He ultimately recommends a radical separation between the spiritual and the temporal to recast the state and rebuild the law according to the requirements of modernity.

Last, Taha Hussayn (1889–1973) arrived in the interwar years with his pro-Western, positivist message, genealogically linked to the Enlightenment. Using the tools of historical literary criticism, he legitimized and authenticated a posteriori the language and myths of the Koran in the creation of the earliest Arabic poetry, anchoring it in the pre-Islamic period.[17] Furthermore, he reminds his fellow Egyptians of their country's role, with Alexandria, in the formation of Greek culture during

one of its later phases, and in that culture's contribution to
Arabic classicism—a double reason to emphasize the sources
that Arabic culture shares with the West.[18] This common root
legitimizes Arab participation in the values of modernity, un-
arguably a product of Europe, notably in spaces opened up by
the Enlightenment philosophers.

Yet we still need to understand why the undeniable effects
of the Enlightenment did not bring about a decisive and practically irreversible change within Islam.[19] The current state of
affairs in Islamic countries demonstrates that the impact of
the Enlightenment was not only insufficient but truly disap-
pointing. Despotism, fanaticism, superstition, obscurantism,
economic impoverishment, underdevelopment, a failure to interiorize the social contract: This is the grim diagnosis that sets
the countries of Islam at a vast remove from Enlightenment
values. I propose at least three reasons for what can only be
called a failure.

First of all, the modernization policies begun in the early
nineteenth century were misguided. Efforts went toward the
assimilation of technical modernization, on the model of Japan's
success story as expressed by its military victory over Russia in
1905. This event held an intense fascination for the people of
Islam, for it proved that technology from the West could be
mastered by a country of the East that could hold on to its
identity and values nonetheless. Yet when this loyalty and self-
reliance went uninflected by Enlightenment values, the Japanese fell into a militarist, fascist brand of nationalism, even
though the Meiji era is linked etymologically to the notion of
light—a term that when used as trope and metaphor obtains
an ambivalent, even suspect multiplicity of meanings.[20] If the
great technological shift is linked historically to a break with
Enlightenment values, we should also note its autonomy,
clearly illustrated by the Japanese case and others, where technology served barbaric ends throughout the twentieth century.
At the same time, it is hard to conceive of Enlightenment values taking root in a society that has not profited from the

material wealth that technology brings. A rise in the level of technology is thus necessary for those values to take hold, but it remains autonomous from them. Hence, the defeat of the Enlightenment is observable both in the success of Japan and in the failure of Islam to assimilate technology.

I will also associate this failure of the Enlightenment with the fear of radical thinking, which advocates break and separation. Enlightenment ideas and principles emerged in opposition to tradition, by making a clean break with the past. The phenomenon was never conceived in accordance with any religious legacy, nor did it even attempt to accommodate religion. The reformers and reformists of Islam never ventured this kind of betrayal; rather, they remained timorously within the bounds of their obsession with loyalty to their faith, which was never confined to a separate space—where it might have remained, anxiously no doubt, as an impregnable secret of the heart. It is as if they feared the commitment as divided subjects fully assuming that division.

Add to all of this, finally, in the late 1920s, anti-Westernism as an ideology of combat elaborated by religious fundamentalists, who rekindled all the traditional refusals, further radicalizing them via Ibn Taymiyyah most notably, and by attempting to hunt down and root out foreign influences that supposedly contaminated a mythic purity. This meant a return to a denunciation of *bida'* (plural of *bid'a*), those innovations to be understood in the most disparaging sense,[21] as negatively overdetermined in the eighteenth century by Ibn 'Abd al-Wahhāb, founder of Wahhabism, whose coercive practices became universal with the influx of petrodollars into Saudi Arabia after the 1973 oil crisis, in an Islamic field left vacant since the defeat of various forms of populist postcolonial nationalism.

Faced with the ebbing of Enlightenment values, I would like to emphasize the role Europe can play in their reactivation. Earlier, I alluded to the hiatus in the West between the notion of Enlightenment and what prevented its becoming universal. But Europeans, in these last few decades of peace, self-awareness, and ethical vigilance, may well be capable of producing acts consistent with their principles. I realize that such exemplarity is difficult to achieve, particularly when it comes to abstracting it from distinctions between strong and weak, rich and poor, powerful and powerless. But by adhering to the principle of justice, it would be tempting to put this exemplarity to the test, to whatever possible and reasonable extent, in this cosmopolitan, postcolonial era. Such a dramatization would offer us the opportunity to restore the prestige of the Enlightenment and its universality by rekindling the flame through Islam. It would require the strong support of those Muslims willing to live with the consequences of those divisions that have plagued the faithful from the start, the war of hierarchies, references, and interpretations—an ongoing civil war, one of whose main issues remains the acquisition of Enlightenment values, reconsidered and corrected according to a mode of thought and experience that would restore the virtues of breaking and separation.

What remains to be tested is civilizing time, and how it gets corrupted throughout history, right down to today's exclusionist Islamic fundamentalists who are abusing civilization's gains. What remains to be tested is that structure that begins with the time of pertinence and ends in the time of powerlessness. This test can be approached by means of two questions that should be of primary concern to us in this cosmopolitan, postcolonial era.

First, it is time to rethink the Enlightenment legacy, to retrace the bounds of its universality, moving beyond (and not suppressing) the critics that would disqualify it, such as Leo Strauss and his followers, who believed that a certain form of Enlightenment worship is destructive to tradition and runs the risk of creating an illusion of assimilation into some falsely universal value system.[22] The Jews of Europe were to pay a heavy price, according to the German-American philosopher: On their road to assimilation as taught to them by Enlightenment values, they ended up helpless before the destructive Nazi forces that denied them those very values. Caught in the confusion of conflict, they were led to their deaths as if by surprise, after having interiorized the idea that the Enlightenment values were a permanent acquisition that finally allowed them to leave behind a millennium of oppression.

This assimilation put forth by Enlightenment principles was adapted to Judaism as early as the eighteenth century by Moses Mendelssohn, who sought to decouple tradition and Law to channel energies toward the positive laws that were gaining ground in the public at large. Mendelssohn advocated a strategy for Judaism to move beyond its own Law, to submit to laws common to all citizens, whatever their belief or origin, a right directly inspired by the Enlightenment. This historical lesson might provide a useful analogy, if not for Islam in general, then at least for Islam within Europe.

Yet this ingenious and necessary adaptation, of great use so long as it remains confined to the juridical and political spheres, becomes detrimental when it precludes the quest for an Absolute, not so much as rituals and forms of worship borne along by belief (which can also become a harmless part of custom), but as "interior experience" that abolishes the scope of sacred and holy (this *espace du dedans*,[23] or "space within," that generates a discourse Georges Bataille calls *hierology* as distinct from theology). My point here is that this was one of the Enlightenment's blind spots not even Voltaire was able to perceive and learn from, even from his reading of Pascal casting his musings like dice on the table of thought, in the fragment that teaches us: "Man forever surpasses Man."[24]

To this double critique, I will add another that I have already referred to on several occasions. It has to do with the emergence of colonialism and slavery in the long view of history, a period during which Western humanity dealt a terrible blow to the very Enlightenment principles it had itself invented.[25] This stark reality contributed to the discrediting of the universality of those values, respected (but not always) in Europe, but neglected or flagrantly violated in faraway lands, in what was later to be termed "overseas."

However, despite the radical critique of the Enlightenment (which I am not evading here), despite the battering of its principles when put to the test of reality, it is important to reconsider these ideas, to renew them so as to put in place a cosmo-politics, viable for the here and now, at this inaugural post-Western moment of history. Thanks to this revised look at the Enlightenment, it might still be possible to neutralize the identity wars being waged in the name of exclusion (a point of agreement between Jacques Derrida and Jürgen Habermas to circumscribe September 11 as a concept[26]) and to revive the premises of its universality in Islam, as I proposed at the start of this chapter.

The second point that concerns our era and the cosmo-politics to come has to do with Nature and the safeguarding of what remains of it in an ailing world, devastated by mindless human action. Here also might be judged the pertinence of tradition in Islamic thought during the centuries when it reigned at the heart of civilization prior to the decline and fall of the consciousness that bids us to live sustainably in the world. During that time, there was a certain way of thinking about Nature, a way of life that left a legacy of knowledge marked by an ethics, a clear forerunner to today's ecological concerns, a destiny that involves us all and one of the major issues on the cosmo-political horizon. The next chapter addresses this topic in more detail.

# CHAPTER 6

# The Physics and Metaphysics of Nature

The notion of nature does not exist in the Bible, any more than it does in the Koran, where it is assimilated to creation. Thus perceived, Nature is a divine gift bestowed upon Man to have dominion over and enjoy. Humans forever marvel before the spectacle of divine Creation, a boundless work founded upon the separation of heaven and earth, light and darkness, day and night.

In the heavens, God placed the sun, the moon, and the stars. Of the earth, he made a stable abode, a bed, a carpet. He raised mountains and created rivers, gardens, and fruits. The winds, which bear beneficial rain, are "good tidings before his mercy" (Koran 7:57). In this manner, the Holy Book renders nature sacred, involving the hand of God in every corner of creation. The divine is manifest everywhere and at every moment. A kind of pantheism emerges from this vision, one that certain spiritual masters of Islam exploited, with the belief that God is immanent, present in nature and person. But let us not get ahead of ourselves here. Before further examining this concept, and to illustrate the constant reference to divine action in

natural phenomena, I will cite the most appropriate and eloquent Koranic verses for the occasion: "Is He not best who created the heavens and the earth and sent down for you rain
from the sky, causing to grow thereby gardens of joyful beauty
which you could not otherwise have grown the trees thereof? . . .
Is He not best who made the earth a stable ground and placed
within it rivers and made for it firmly set mountains and placed
between the two seas a barrier?" (Koran 27:60–61).

At the risk of appearing to digress, I should like to point out
that this enigmatic "barrier" or "isthmus" (the Koranic term
being *barzakh*, a word of Persian origin[1]) would later take on the
meaning of a spiritual topography, the *barzakh* being the intermediary space where creative imagination is at work. It is also
the middle passage that welcomes the dead awaiting resurrection on Judgment Day. But such spiritual and eschatological
considerations divert us from what I intend to focus on here.
Before returning to the reference to the garden, it might be useful to recall the importance of water, whose benefits are so often
extolled in the Koran. The Holy Book emerged in a desert milieu, where dryness and water shortage are the rule. No surprise,
then, that the least presence of water is associated with the
miracle of the origin of life. "The heavens and the earth were a
joined entity, and We separated them and made from water every
living thing" (Koran 21:30). This verse is often written out in calligraphy to celebrate the tapping of springs, the building of
dams, and the creation of public fountains in both town and
countryside. But beyond the link to ecology, beyond the influence of milieu on the written word, or even the spoken pro-
nouncements of an oracle, this verse expresses a biological
principle that resonates with Thales de Miletus, the pre-Socratic
physiologist: "Water is the principle of all things, and God is
that Mind which shaped and created all things from water."[2]

This predilection for water was also expressed within the Islamic city, where it would become an important issue in the
exercise of power. Beside Karl Wittfogel's claim that water was
the basis for "oriental despotism,"[3] this vital element provided

material for law and jurisprudence, owing to the dissension that arose when water was shared out in agricultural irrigation systems. In cities like Valencia even today, a special court for water distribution issues is still held in front of the cathedral every Thursday at noon, a surprising Islamic relic maintained by *Levante* folklore. Moreover, water management evolved into a sophisticated technology, as demonstrated in Spain by numerous mechanic's manuals that are used by the few *norias*, or bucket elevators, still in use, which employ age-old Arab technology, as is the case with the enormous waterwheel located in the *huerta* of Murcia, not far from the town. It is worth noting that to this day, irrigation in Spain perpetuates the legacy of the Islamic period. A good part of the lexicon concerning its techniques derives from Arabic. And although the surviving network of the Valencia *huerta* is not in itself an Arab creation, it still should be noted that the principles underpinning its conception and distribution are indeed of Arab origin.

I could also mention the water reserves located directly outside the ramparts of old cities, such as Kairouan in Tunisia, where the immense Aghlabid pools provide a welcome cooling effect during the hot summer months, when soaring temperatures bring life to a standstill. In the crushing summer heat, the sensual effect provided by water is at least as important as its more functional role. The same can be said for that other scorching city of Western Islam, Marrakesh, which offers visitors magnificent pools of water at Agdal and especially at Menara.[4] All around Marrakesh, I saw the remains of *foggarāt*, underground canals covered by earthen vaults that channeled water to the city from springs and Atlas Mountains snowmelt. In these same outskirts of Marrakesh, I visited the town of Tamesloht in the company of Mohammed El Faiz, who showed me the remains of one of these underground channels that is extended by an aqueduct whose elevation is ingeniously designed so that the water can climb the slope and arrive at its destination with enough pressure, thanks to a system of communicating vessels.

Water also circulates within the cities, on the one hand, to feed fountains considered charitable works celebrated by monuments that mix stone and mosaic, wood and marble, polychrome highlights and calligraphy; but this water also serves *intra muros* gardens. Cairene *sabils* feature marble slabs sculpted in a wavelike pattern, lending to the solid material the fluidity of liquid. In Fes, until very recently, the water network was dense: Rivulets followed the sloping streets; certain channels passed through the patios of houses and madrassas; water flowed through the city via two distinct networks—clean drinking water and wastewater. In his sixteenth-century *Description d'Afrique*, Leo Africanus was already giving an account of the considerable network there, part buried, part open air, as it powered water mills, fed public baths or hammams, or provided water for ablutions in mosques and *zawiyas* or shrines. This water worship does not correspond only to some naturalist or vitalist exaltation; rather, it is also associated with the ritual purity that obsesses the faithful, a prerequisite to prayer or reading of the Holy Book. Ablutions, major or minor, always involve the contact of water and the body to wash away secretions and excrement considered as a stain (breaking wind, urine, fecal matter, sperm, menstrual blood). It is worth noting that in the traditional hierarchy, the guild of workers in charge of cleaning out and maintaining these canals was considered the lowliest, inferior to even tanners.[5]

It is impossible to talk about water without mentioning gardens. The two are already associated in the Koran, along with the extolling of shade. Here again, we can assume that the existence of gardens corresponds to a vision of the oasis, the mirage of the desert dweller, already sublimated in the Koran where it represents the promise of the mythic Eden. In a certain way, the creation of the garden is experienced as an anticipation, an earthly foretaste of paradise. For Islam is a religion that does not suppress the body but lends a physical reality to promise and punishment through emphasis on the sensual and the carnal, a point that was often raised in the disputes and polemics among believers of the single, undivided God during the period of cohabitation among the three monotheisms.[6] The garden is a place of delight, of complete sensual enjoyment, achieved through the conjunction of water, trees, and shade. The entire body is attuned to the music of the water as it gushes, flows, and cascades, gurgles, sings, and whispers, or falls one droplet at a time. Visually, the colors of the garden dance, wave upon wave, like paper lanterns swaying in trees. And the fine fragrances are breathed in and soothe all our organs like a beverage, while shade itself takes on a character, becomes as palpable as a being.

Water worship achieves one of its most eloquent architectural expressions in Grenada, at the Alhambra palace and in the Generalife gardens. The pools located within the building complex itself are meant to exalt the architectural forms and ornaments that reflect into the colorless water like a mirror. This is the case for the stalactite-studded dome whose image is reproduced in the pool of one of the lateral rooms, called "The Hall of the Two Sisters," adjacent to the Court of the Lions. These sculpted beasts, twelve in all and arranged in a circle, produce a kind of music with the water flowing from their mouths. Around the rim of the fountain supported by the lions is inscribed a poem that exalts with words what the senses are already experiencing, the sights, sounds, and even the feel of the air and the light. The poem emphasizes the cosmic scope of this display, where all the elements join together. Water from the fountain, the earthen bricks, the fiery light, the limpid air all combine to create a play of illusions between real and virtual, where solid walls take on a liquid appearance and their opacity itself assumes the translucency of light.

But I have to say that the miracle of water is celebrated to the utmost degree by the *scala d'aqua* of the Generalife, a nonfunctional, purely gratuitous act that channels water along the gradual slope of the ramp dug in such a way as to generate a musical rhythm that alternates fast and slow sequences depending on the varying degrees of the slope. This channel runs along an elaborate set of steps, where landings provide a moment's rest and the water slows down along with the climber. Thus, the movement of water becomes music, combing different tempos to match our human rhythms, from allegretto to presto, and all the tempi in between. Water evokes a double analogy, poetic and musical, in the gardens of Grenada. The music orchestrated by the water stairs of Generalife infuses the soul with joy in the presence of beauty, and calms the troubled mind with its shades of sound.

The garden could well be the reward earned by the desert dwellers who swept across North Africa to settle in this more temperate climate. It is not by chance that Spain offered the ideal dwelling place marked by the Edenic promise of a natural setting that unfailingly reproduced its miracles, its divine gifts. The Arab poets of Andalusia praised these places of enchantment, which to this day are well maintained and put to use, as testify the Partal of Grenada, the gardens of Seville and the Crucero, of the Alcazar and the Casa Pilatos. Among these many poets, I will mention Ibn Khafāja, native of Levante, in the Valencia region. He lived between the eleventh and twelfth centuries, and was nicknamed the *jannān*, or gardener.[7] His descriptions contributed greatly to feeding the myth of Andalusia. In his poems, he bestows a soul upon plant life and projects characters onto the elements, granting them human gestures borrowed from the pleasures that enliven the meeting of Dionysus and Eros, where music prompts dancing:

> Flowers, polished as mirrors, their stems bend
> In the fragrant breeze that wraps around their corolla.
> There, among them, a bewitching cup-bearer, body of ebony,
> Jet-black eyes, ardent love, serving the russet libation.
> A necklace of flowers, branches like strands of hair;
> The vale a wrist, the river a bracelet.
> In a garden where red shade contrasts with the white
> Of flowers, lips part showing a flash of teeth,
> And the earth drank, the long reed danced,
> The dove sang, the stream applauded.[8]

Concomitantly, horticultural literature in Arabic also prospered in Spain, especially under the Taïfa kings (eleventh–twelfth c.).[9] This corpus grew steadily with an Arabic translation of the famous Latin agronomist Junius Columella of Gades (Cádiz). Most of the treatises handed down to us follow an outline based on the model of *De re rustica*. The authors in question were either physicians or poets. Rarely were they agronomists. In this regard, it is worth recalling that Aristotle was as much a naturalist as a creator of botanical gardens, and that it was Virgil who wrote the *Georgics*. In any event, it is highly likely that the Hispano-Arab authors knew and made use of the authors of antiquity. They added their own observations and personal experimentation. This kind of literary burgeoning corresponds to Islam's duality, which ranges from attitudes inherited from its desert origins to the adaptation to Mediterranean traditions. It is important to temper the perceived clash of civilizations, and rather to focus on the continuities that the Mediterranean has shared over the centuries. Certain of these treatises were translated into various Romance languages during the Middle Ages. And it was in eleventh-century Muslim Spain that the first royal botanical gardens appeared in Europe, in Toledo and then in Seville. These were both pleasure gardens and test gardens, intended to acclimatize plants brought over from the East.

Extending the principle of the Roman farm, heralding the civilization of villas that the Venetian and Florentine Renaissance would experience, Arab Spain came up with an intermediary formula that blended the townhouse and the country residence, one that clearly delineated the functions of the vacation home and those related to agricultural activities. In the 157th and final chapter of the *Treatise on Agriculture* composed in verse by Ibn Luyūn of Almeria (fourteenth c.),[10] the living quarters are described as surrounded by decorative plants and evergreen trees with thick foliage. They open onto a portico, which then gives onto an enclosed garden, longer than it is wide, where flowerbeds and ponds alternate, with rivulets of water running throughout. At the center of this ideal garden is built a shady gazebo that allows for an unobstructed 360-degree view of the surrounding garden. The orchard and vegetable garden are located outside this enclosure, while the stables for horses and draft animals, as well as animals raised for consumption, are relegated to an even more remote location.

If I have evoked Muslim Spain in such glowing terms, it is because it experienced a nearly miraculous level of civilization, and it remains near and dear to me as an intermediary stopping point, a restorative stage between my native African, Maghrebi soil and my Parisian, European place of residence. But I could just as well have undertaken my study in Abbasid Baghdad, where I would have called attention to the gardens of Kharq lauded by the poets; I could have gone on at length about the poems of Buhturī (died in 897), who described the palaces and gardens of Mesopotamia, or entered the Persian domain inspired by the Sassanid tradition, as illustrated by albums of illuminations and miniatures. Pushing further east and back in time, how could I omit the achievements in the art of gardens among the great Moguls? Nor could I fail to mention the special place of the Ottomans in the history of horticulture, the culture of tulips in particular, of which they produced 839 varieties in the eighteenth century. Truly, in this area as in others, the peoples and nations that joined Islam adapted their own traditions to the recommendations and images contained in the Koranic crucible. This articulation will allow us to decipher the variety and unity of artistic activities in the Islamic milieu.

In the representation of the Koranic promise with regard to gardens, man imitates divine creation. The garden is the ideal, reiterating the miracle. By concentrating the marvels of nature in an enclosed and specially arranged space, the initiate is better able to glean material for the elaboration of his spiritual exercises. I will always remember the magnificent sixteenth-century Persian painting, conserved in the Louvre, that depicts a young ephebe completely absorbed in the contemplation of a narcissus.[11] This image can be admirably interpreted by referring to

Ibn 'Arabī's theory of Being. Commenting on a work from the sixteenth century by means of a thirteenth-century text might appear aberrant from the historical standpoint. But one must bear in mind that cultural time in Islamic civilization is different from that of the West where, with the break that took place in the Middle Ages, styles and schools followed each other in rapid succession. Ibn 'Arabī, although he wrote in Arabic, was born in Murcia, Spain, at the western extreme of Islamic territoriality, and came three hundred years before, continued to be read and commented on in sixteenth-century Persia. His conception of the oneness of Being was universally accepted there. The contemplation of the flower is in fact an actualization of the whole process of Creation. Like all natural manifestations, the flower is an epiphany, a *tajallī*. It is a trace descended from the Tablet. Ibn 'Arabī asks us to imagine the conjunction of all the cosmic movement required for such a descent to take place. So much coordination among the winds, the rains, daylight and darkness, the months, the seasons, on the one hand, and the governance of Man on the other, that the flower sign laid down on the celestial Tablet marks its trace in the order of beings here below.[12] The orant, through the mental operation of contemplation, travels the descending path in the opposite direction. He moves backward, from the trace manifested on the face of the world toward the sign inscribed on the Tablet in the heavens. In a second stage, he recollects the creative process through which the flower sign, like any sign, gets inscribed onto the Tablet at the beginning, and in the principle. This inscription is achieved after a perfect circuit of communication, either the active, emitting pole represented by the first created instance, the Intellect, visualized by the writing implement, or *qalam*; or a passive receiver, the universal Soul, materialized by the Tablet. It is the conjunction of these two figures that will engender the third term, the sign inscribed subsequent to the divine fiat ("When He decrees a matter, He only says to it, 'Be,' and it is,"[13] Koran 2:117, along with six other instances). Creation is thus understood as an act of writing that is also a metaphor of love, where a masculine is joined to a feminine in order that an engendering take place. And the manifestation of being is no other than the copy, the reproduction of what was transcribed at the beginning. The world is therefore the book of the Book. It is through these copies of the Book deposited in the fragments of nature that Being can be deciphered.[14]

Man, created in the image of God, is his successor on earth, as the Koran emphasizes, for Man in general, and as addressed to David in particular.[15] The term used in Arabic, *khalīfa*, adapted into English as "caliph" or successor, designates only the political institution and function (invented upon the succession of the Prophet, at Medina), with no consideration for the moral valence that links all humans (*nāsūt*) to the divine (*lāhūt*). From this perspective, man's vocation is not simply to enjoy the divine work of nature. He also is assigned the task of governance. Any lapse in this duty is perceived as a profanation.

I will refer once again to a Spanish writer to illustrate this arrangement, the famous twelfth-century philosopher and physician, Ibn Tufayl, born near Grenada and died in Marrakesh. His philosophical novel, *Hayy Ibn Yaqzan* (which depicts a man living alone on a desert island, inspired by an older Arab tale, and which would in turn inspire Baltasar Gracián's *Criticón*[16]) contains pages where nature worship leans more toward a functionalist attitude closer to today's ecological awareness than to romantic effusiveness.[17] After having discovered God, through both logical deduction and inspiration, after admitting the coherence of Being under the aegis of the One, after establishing man's divine line of descent with regard to the moral pact, Hayy, thanks to his skill and dexterity, declares himself protector of plants and animals to affirm the continuity of the living (which is, moreover, the meaning of his name, Hayy, which means "alive, living"). His intervention in the world tempers the inevitable disturbance of the natural order. To the extent possible, it must contribute to the thriving of all living things. It is up to him to remove anything that deprives a plant of sunshine; he is to separate plants that mingle and do one another harm, to protect animals harassed by wild beasts, or even to relieve their cuts and scratches caused by sharp foreign objects, such as thorns or splinters, which they cannot remove on their own. He is also to clear the course of streams that will then irrigate trees. And finally, in accordance with the strict rules of an ascetic ideal and a concern for the furtherance of species, he must limit his consumption of natural products to only what is necessary for his own survival.

While the merger of nature and Creation is not questioned by the believer, while it is sublimated by the poet and artist, exalted by the mystic and perpetuated by the protagonist of philosophical fiction, we have already seen that it is, if not surpassed, then at least circumvented by the naturalist, who activates his reason and sense of observation via the system of classification borrowed from the ancient Mesopotamians, Greeks, and Latins, transmitted notably by two treatises translated into Arabic in the tenth century (*L'Agriculture nabatéenne*[18] and *L'Agriculture grecque*). But it is especially the *Traité des simples* by the Spaniard Ibn al-Baythar (thirteenth c.) that gathered into a single work what we owe to Dioscorides and Galen, as well as to Avicenna and Rāzī, and to a number of his contemporaries. It also contains the author's personal inquiry carried out in Andalusia and in the Maghreb, Egypt, and Syria. This summa, which remained unsurpassed until the sixteenth century, was translated by Antoine Galland in the early eighteenth century (a translation that went unnoticed), and more notably by Lucien Leclerc in 1878.[19] This work is an admirable illustration of how Arabic as a language participates in the scientific corpus based on a spirit of practicality and the sense of observation and classification. This is a far cry from metaphysical speculation or revealed sources that deny the existence of nature as autonomous. In fact, the issue of the relationship between nature and Creation is not even raised, and with this omission the concept of nature becomes self-evident. But it had to be named. There was thus an urgent need to broaden the meaning of the word *tabīʿa* (which etymologically means "innate feature") to include physics and life sciences. This same word, in modern standard Arabic, designates the equivalent of "nature" in all its many meanings, and in the very broadest sense, which is to say, "the external world in its entirety" (*Merriam-Webster's Collegiate Dictionary*). Usage has meant that this word has prevailed over the one used in the Koran, *fitra*,[20] which refers to that which belongs to human beings before anything gets imprinted upon them, in other words, at birth.[21] This term defines man's condition as we suppose it was prior to any civilization. The word is still used whenever the distinction between nature and culture is made.

Hence, the anthropological and historical reality of Arab man remains ambivalent. Which of the two meanings put forward above (which have led me to interrupt the logic of my presentation in order to situate the interiorizing of the garden between the geoponic and the hermeneutic) takes precedence over the other? Does experience corroborate the poet's hymn or the gardener's sequencing? Does it confirm the mystic's contemplation and interpretation? Does it honor the philosopher's pantheism? Does it submit to the observations and taxonomy of the naturalist? Does it at least remain faithful to the model laid down in the Koranic matrix? Here again, once the question is posed with regard to a specific domain, we are faced with the same question that Islam has constantly had to confront: Which of the two standpoints prevails? Or do they alternate, can they exist simultaneously, side by side within the same person? What have Arabs opted for? For a separation of the entities of nature and Creation that would emphasize scientific progress? For a merging of the two that would render poetic and sacred the enjoyment of being in the world? For both, depending on the need of the moment? It is clear that Islam still must think this issue through, and either move in the direction of continuity or opt to break with the tradition set in motion by the Greeks.

I would like to include another text in our collection. It is the *Calendar of Cordova*, which appeared in the eleventh century.[22] Its Arabic is clearly inflected by accents from the *Georgics*. A practical work, its closeness to nature unleashes a kind of pagan energy. Attentive to the natural cycles of work and time, the book marks the duration of nighttime and the length of shadows according to the passage of the months. Adhering to the description of the solar cycle, the treatise makes mention of religious feast days that mark the calendar, even when they are foreign, that is, Christian. In fact, this presence has authorized some historians to attribute the calendar in question to two Christian authors. I prefer to see two hands at work, one Muslim, the other Christian, which would correspond to a more fruitful effect of Andalusia's interfaith cohabitation and the hospitality granted by the Islamic city when ruled by a power capable of welcoming difference. In any event, the Arabic-language work takes account of many Catholic saints' feast days and the major fixed-date holidays, such as the Nativity and the Assumption, as well as more mobile commemorations whose dates vary according to solar and lunar calculations, such as Jewish Passover and Christian Holy Week.

The calendar registers daily observations with regard to the movement of heavenly bodies, the waxing and waning hours of day and night, weather trends, the work patterns of peasants, or such state-sponsored activities as tax collecting or military enrollment. This treatise also suggests ways to seek relief from seasonal extremes—hot or cold, wet or dry. By way of example, here is the passage that concludes the chapter devoted to the month of February, a quote that blends information and noteworthy events of day-to-day existence:

> Baby birds are hatching, bees are reproducing, water creatures are starting to move again, women are beginning to incubate their silkworm cocoons, cranes are returning to the islands. Saffron bulbs are being planted, as well as summer vegetables. Many trees are sprouting leaves. Truffles, wild asparagus and fennel are abundant. It is time to graft the pear and apple trees. Vineyards are being planted, as are fallen buds. We are now permitted to be bled, and to consume medications—as long as they are not too strong—should the need arise. During this month, letters are sent with the purpose

of recruiting for summer campaigns. Swallows and storks have returned to the cities.

This calendar describing the days of the year in Andalusia
does at times refer to phenomena that take place in Arabia during the same period. Does this kind of reference to a land of
origin (which is at very least the land of the language in which
the calendar is written) suggest another ambivalence, expressing an attachment to a spatial duality where the real country is
shadowed by a mythical homeland? What is certain, in any
case, is that this calendar implicitly reveals the double tempo-
rality that pervades the Islamic consciousness. Indeed, it makes
perfect sense that the Hijrī counting system is not used in a
calendar meant to adapt human activities to a relationship
with nature based on the logic of the seasons. Thus, the Muslim is confronted, on the one hand, with a sacred and liturgical
time that depends on the lunar cycle, and which, in its mobil-
ity, locates important dates along an ever-shifting slide of seasons. On the other, the Muslim deals in a time meant for worldly
and political activities that do not escape the immutability of the
solar cycle. This ambivalence where the perception of time is
marked by two different cycles makes it impossible to merge the
two. The separation of time into sacred and profane constitutes a
fact that can be transfigured only by the hermeneutic of the oneness of Being. But what of a divided consciousness, split in its
representation of time? Divided between inconstant sister moon
and unshakable brother sun, Islamic humanity turns with the
wheel of time, changing the viewing angle through which it
gazes at the night sky. The temporal round thus uses the same
orbit, passing by the same stations, but the roundabout is enlivened by an opening, itself always in motion, that varies in duration and intensity depending on the place it occupies.

This is only an archaeological sketch of the sentiment of nature in Islam. It is a plausible construction in its very ambivalence.
But what remains of such considerations, whose documentary
material dates no later than the thirteenth century, apart from a

few furtive mentions up to the eighteenth century, broadening the topic upon encounter with the Ottomans, the Safavids, and the Moguls? We know that historical amnesia can be devastating, especially when it is not experienced as such. We also know that all civilization survives between its constructions and their destruction. This pattern is all the more pronounced in Arab history, where founding is followed in rapid succession by deposition, further exacerbated, perhaps, by the reality, if not the persistence, of nomadic life. One idea at the heart of the cyclical vision of history developed by Ibn Khaldūn in the fourteenth century involves the opposition between nomads and sedentary peoples as key to the evolution of human societies. "When the Arabs descend upon a place, it will soon be ruined" (*idhā 'urribat khurribat*). Every human establishment is threatened with destruction by entities on the move, whether conquering hordes or simply nomads. Every garden is a potential target for pillaging. Cataclysms are not only so-called natural phenomena, but also man-made. Man leaves lasting traces on the earth's crust. The arid conditions of the African steppe (today's Tunisia), for instance, have been blamed on the twelfth-century invasion of the Banū Hilāl, nomadic tribes originating in Arabia, sent by the Fatimid caliph of Cairo to punish the insubordination of his Berber allies.[23] This hypothesis can serve as a model, though some scholars find it excessive.

It might well be that we are currently in a period of experiencing the harmful effects of the nomadic existence, at least with regard to nature and sustainability. The curse of underdevelopment, made worse by demographic pressure, has resulted in the abandonment of the wasted countryside and a population explosion in urban centers. This movement could be considered a modern form of nomadism. The early effects that appear mark a break rather than a fresh start. In societies already trending toward oblivion and which no longer control the movements of their population, the little that is saved of tradition begins to break up, and consciousness, however divided, obsesses over its slow, seemingly endless agony, the sign of a time of crisis. It is probably at this crisis point that attitudes of solidarity with nature begin to fall apart. I won't get into denouncing the long list of misguided development efforts that include environmentally harmful projects, unlawful in more enlightened countries that have come to protect nature while pursuing their development, but I will mention at least one: the chemical plants in Gabès, southern Tunisia, that destroyed the palm grove of the only maritime oasis in the world, which is now completely sterile. Worse than this, however, is the incomprehensible violence against nature at the individual level. It is here that the true loss and deep-seated amnesia can be assessed. Confronted with the huge material means of industry, we can reasonably grasp how classic structures and genealogies can be buried and forgotten. But how to fathom people's aggression against trees on a daily basis in dry countries, under a punishing sun? I am filled with a sense of unease and strangeness when faced with acts by humans who have relinquished their faculty of discrimination (*al-quwwa al-mumayyiza*)[24] to the point where the very people mortally threatened by the pounding sun no longer seem to remember the virtue of the shade tree and the cooling it provides. At home, the triumph of cement has destroyed the love of gardens. The argument of survival eclipses all aesthetic concerns, nature's guardians. The meaning borne aloft by the voice that declaims the Book is no longer heard, even when amplified by crackly loudspeakers. All that remains is the unbearable violence of evil, which extends its reach while the little that survives of classical attitudes disappears, to the detriment of the Middle Sea: the Mediterranean that has become a dumping ground for plastic refuse bearing trademarks in countless graphics (Latin letters, or Greek, Arabic, or Cyrillic, or Eastern ideograms), the broken tablets of a rotting Babel, crumbling into ruin. What a heroic task it would be to gather up this detritus and bury it in a monumental tomb, around which would circumambulate the pilgrims of a new faith!

## Epilogue: Religion and Cosmopolitics

Andalusia, with its three cultures, has often been evoked as a moment when Islam, Christianity, and Judaism were able to live and thrive together. Without falling into the vision of a golden age of history that filters out violence and conflict, I must acknowledge that this entente did take place and that it produced recognizable vestiges, a few examples of which we have brought to mind here. One need only survey the architectural legacy to be convinced of the fact, for it is the most visible proof of a shared community within the city, a semiotics to be read as a way of being and feeling that brings together differences beneath heavens of a shared identity.

Indeed, many edifices belonging to the three religions shared the same system of signs, adapted to the ritual and cultural requirements that distinguish synagogue, mosque, and church. The cohabitation of the sacred letters within the same space is what I elect as symbol of this *convivence*. For example, both Hebrew and Arabic are found in the synagogue of Transito, as I mentioned earlier. To this instance, let us add another monument in Toledo, the Church of San Román, consecrated in 1221, whose horseshoe-shaped arches—creating a very Islamic profile—are inscribed in both Arabic and Latin calligraphy. Here, the cultural mix is even more moving, with frescoes alongside the typically Moorish poly-lobed bays. The result is a paradoxical space where an Islamic decor welcomes Christian religious paintings that exhibit saints, prophets, and scenes from the Apocalypse.

This style, called *mudejar* art, is hybrid style at its finest. Examples of it occur here and there throughout cities, visible during walks through Seville, for instance, a city whose campaniles display ornaments inspired by the Almohad *sebka*, a grid of rhombuses, a geometric network of trellises, diamond shapes, and ribbing that migrated from embroidery to masonry, from threadwork to stone and brick. It expanded to include the facets of the Almohad minaret of Giralda, whose main decorative motif would also grace the towers of San Pedro, San Marco, Santa Catalina, the Omnium Sanctorum, and so on. All these bell towers bear a resemblance to minarets, even in their shapes, which, according to the western Mediterranean Islamic tradition, are built on a square plan articulated around a central core.

Yet this cohabitation of religions and styles was taking place at a time when religious exclusivity among nations was the order of the day. What then of today, when communication has generalized widespread cultural exchange, when vast tracts of the globe have been deeply marked by Westernization and secularization? Such exchange and awareness raising should be made all the easier, and should be included, for instance, in the pedagogical programs of states worldwide, in consonance with Rousseau, who recommended that the state be "the people's teacher."

But in order to accomplish such a task, we will have to take the path back to the texts, which, in each of the three religious traditions, conclude that behind religions in the plural, there is always "religion" in the singular. Without seeking to evade the issue of particularism that underpins each belief system, it is important to rediscover within each separate religion the truth of what might be called the first religion. Again, this is a notion inherited from the Enlightenment. Along with Rousseau, we can look to Kant's perspective on this question.

It is Kant's view that the diversity of religions is what not only prevents peoples from mixing but precipitates their separation in the first place. It hinders the advent of the cosmo-political era for which he was attempting to prepare the way. But Kant interrupts his own reasoning process and, in a note, backtracks a bit to contest the accepted meaning of the formula: "Diversity of religions—a singular expression! It is precisely as if one spoke of different moralities. There may very well be different kinds of historical faiths attached to different means employed in the promotion of religion, and indeed, these belong to the field of learned investigation. Similarly there may be different religious texts (Zendavesta, the Veda, the Koran, etc.), but such differences do not exist in religion, there being only one religion valid for all men and in all ages. These can, therefore, be nothing else than accidental vehicles of religion, thus changing with times and places."[1]

Religion thus proves artificial and illusory, though it is the cause of so much human dissension, sedition, division, hatred, war, and violence—the death instinct of Thanatos, in other words—that has brought down so many civilizations.

This notion seems to have been born of Enlightenment logic, which is so explicitly expressed in the atmosphere opened up by the cosmo-political outlook. Yet we find that it had already germinated in the minds of a far earlier people, less enlightened in appearance, or at least theocentric and not yet secularized. If we look a few centuries back, we will indeed discover these forerunners, namely the Catholic Nicholas Cusanus (1401–64), the Jew Moshe Ibn 'Ezra (c. 1060–1135), and the Muslim Ibn 'Arabī (1164–1240).

The first example is invaluable, for this German author brings together the philosopher and the man of the Church, the freethinker and the cardinal, a close friend to popes. Against the backdrop of the war against the Turks, intensified by the fall of Constantinople (May 29, 1453), did he not write *On the Peace of Faith* (De pace fidei), which advocated eternal peace instead of religious wars, since all humans have but one and the same faith whose formulas and ceremonies differ? Philosophers, he says, have a role to play with regard to their communities and peoples by demonstrating that their religion, apart from its dogmas and rites, is comparable to the religion of reason that all humans share. In this way, peace could be guaranteed.

In order to reach a reasonable agreement intended to "establish a perpetual peace in religion,"[2] Nicholas Cusanus brings foreigners into dialogue with the representatives of his own faith: the holy Word, Paul and Peter. They receive a succession of outside interlocutors: the Arab, the Jew, the Indian, the Persian, the Chaldean, the Tartar, the Bohemian, the Turk, the Armenian, and the Greek, alongside figures more familiar to Germans, such as the Frenchman, the Englishman, the Italian, or the Spaniard. That each of these is granted his say already honors the conditions of universal hospitality established by Kant to ensure his perpetual peace, which is not a mark of philanthropy but rather a right of the foreigner, who is not to be treated as an enemy. This is to be taken as a right not of residence but of temporary sojourn.[3] Which seems to be the modus operandi for the theatrical encounter proposed by Nicholas Cusanus.

How then to preserve peace against this contest for the truth that diversity engenders? One need only come to agreement on a single common rule: Since salvation is linked to belief, each person's faith will be considered safe. "Despite the diversity of rites, the peace of faith remains nevertheless inviolate."[4] With faith and peace ensured, ceremonies and rites would enter into a healthy competition that would engender emulation among the believers of various faiths. Thus, rivalry among religions would maintain the religious core they all share in common, the one that brings them together.[5] It is incumbent upon the wise men of each community to guide the believers toward a single form of worship. Then they will meet up in Jerusalem to accept a single faith and found upon it "a perpetual peace."[6]

You will have noted, then, that the Kantian expression "perpetual peace" had already appeared in the mid–fifteenth century, penned by Cusanus, twice over, at the beginning and at the end of his text, in the first and in the sixty-eighth and final paragraph. In a way, the expression frames the discourse, launching it and bringing it to a close, representing both the sun's rising and setting, as if to herald the Kantian elaboration. And from this fifteenth-century text, we receive a precious gift in the form of the vocation granted to Jerusalem, that great bone of contention, already perceived as a rallying point and symbol of conciliation, the holy city that once again might well serve the function of religious capital of the coming cosmo-political order.

As for Moshe Ibn 'Ezra, whom we have already encountered in an earlier section of this book, he does not really present an explicit theory of the oneness of religion among a diversity of creeds. Yet we can infer this stance from the way he gives credit to a belief foreign to his own. As a Jew, he respects the Islamic belief and takes it seriously. He quotes the Koran (which he calls *Qur'ān al-'Arab*,[7] or the Koran of the Arabs) alongside, and as valid as, the Bible (which he calls *Kitābuna al-Muqaddas*, or Our Holy Book). His knowledge of the sacred book of Islam is sufficient for him to consider one of the dogmas regarding the Koran, the one that affirms its rhetorical inimitability, as a sign of its authenticity, its "unsurpassable" nature, the notion of *'ijāz* that I evoked in chapter 2. Ibn 'Ezra believes it is not his place to counter this claim, while at the same times he does cite Muslim thinkers who sought to undermine it, particularly al Ma'arrī in his *Al-Fuçūl wa 'l-Ghāyāt* (Paragraphs and Periods).[8]

Ibn 'Ezra also describes a period of exceptional felicity for Jews that in his view lasted some thirty-five years in Grenada, as experienced a generation before his by fellow Jew Ibn Nagrila (993–1056),[9] who was prime minister to the Zirid emir Bādīs for a period of sixteen years. At the time of the Tā'ifa kingdoms, this emir had extended his authority over the city and surrounding territories. Ibn 'Ezra confirms that Ibn Nagrila, a native of Mérida, studied in Cordova and then became a statesman in Grenada. Under his authority, we acknowledge what was probably the most glorious moment in the history of Jews in exile prior to the era of democracy and assimilation induced by the Enlightenment, which, after the trauma of the Shoah, led them to settle successfully in the United States.[10] Ibn Nagrila was also a military commander and, as such, was to conduct military campaigns on behalf of his Muslim prince. Moreover, he was perfectly fluent in Arabic and in all the religious and profane sciences necessary for the optimal exercise of power in an Islamic city. We note here not only the functional dimension but also the credit granted to the religion and law of the other. In the text of Ibn 'Ezra that reports these facts and events, we spot proof that he intuits the oneness of religion beneath the religious diversity symbolized by the gap between Islam and Judaism, when it comes to worship, ceremony, and rite.

Ibn Nagrila was also a poet, and he excelled in the application of Arabic prosody (the *'arūd*) to Hebrew, in which he wrote poems with themes ranging from the Bacchic to the elegiac, from epic to liturgical. This propensity toward excellence in both chant and warfare led him to think that he was the David of his time.

As stated above, in order to better serve the Islamic power, he had to interiorize the *sharī'a*, or Islamic Law, though this did not prevent him from pointing out certain contradictions contained in the Koran, with remarks consigned to an opus that provoked a violent reaction from Ibn Hazm, "an unbounded aggressiveness,"[11] sparing neither Ibn Nagrila himself, nor his community, nor the Holy Book that served as his guide and reference. In this frightful polemic, which reflects badly on its author in the end, only the call for bodily harm was avoided, in the name of the *dhimmi*'s right to protection, which, according to Ibn Hazm, should not go beyond the inferior rank conceded to him. It may well be that the acrimoniousness of the reply had more to do with the glory surrounding Ibn Nagrila, which distanced him from what would normally have been the humbled *dhimmi* position that the orthodoxy embodied by Ibn Hazm imposed upon Jews, among others.

Still, Ibn Nagrila was ever vigilant and kept close watch over the interests of his community. Under his government, the city experienced a high point of civilization: Science and technology, arts and letters, all flourished as a result of Jews and Arabs living together in the same community under the authority of Berber princes, who extended the city toward a hillside known as Gharnatat al-Yahūd, or Jewish Granada.

Taking up once more the Kantian formulas qualifying the welcome of foreigners within the bounds of cosmo-political hospitality, we can assume that this Jewish segment of mid–eleventh-century Grenada went beyond the visitor's rights that foreigners can claim, to obtain the right of residence.

Let us now go back to Ibn 'Arabī, who advocated nothing less than the religious cohabitation inferred by religious oneness within the diversity of forms of belief. He astutely theorizes the dialectic tension between the One and the many, which is expressed through a single religion translated into a plurality of worship. The paths leading to God are many, but all take on an incontestable legitimacy in his eyes. He even manages to positively interpret idolatry via certain material in the Koran, even though it would seem at first glance irredeemably negative.[12]

For Ibn ʿArabī, the initiate knows that, whatever one's belief, it is God who is adored: No matter what form we lend Him, it is He who is represented. "The distinction (*tafrīq*) and the multitude (*kathra*) of beliefs are like the members of sensitive forms and like the faculties of the soul in a person. Thus, none other than God is adored, no matter the worship."[13] The God of the various beliefs is fabricated by the very ones that contemplate him in adoration. Thus, in praising him, they are praising themselves, which is the reason why they denigrate the beliefs of others. We need to become conscious that the exclusive claims made by religions stem from a narcissistic impulse. To believe in a belief other than one's own amounts to entering into the experience of otherness, getting outside oneself, instantiating oneself face-to-face with another that one speaks and listens to. This is why it is appropriate to know God in all forms and through all beliefs, for God is in the *zann* (opinion, supposition) of believers: he is what they believe he is. Thus, Ibn ʿArabī has God say: "I am wherever my worshiper believes I am."[14] One thus approaches God on the basis of conjecture.

This attitude inspired Ibn ʿArabī with the following lines:

The belief of creatures in God are many
And I testify to everything in which they believe.

This is the emblem that authorizes Ibn ʿArabī to freely exercise his visitor's rights, making him a Muslim wandering among beliefs. He dwells awhile in their abode to enjoy the pertinence of each belief, without seeking to evade or reduce beliefs to the unthinkable notions or taboos cultivated in his own community. We saw in an earlier chapter what he made of his "visit" to Christianity, and how he praised the notion of the Trinity, how inconophilia radiates from the heart of it.

In the end, of course, Moshe Ibn ʿEzra, Nicholas Cusanus, and Ibn ʿArabī all do give precedence to their own creed. First of all, Ibn ʿEzra ended up having to leave Grenada in 1096 when the Almoravids brought down the Zirid principality. These Berbers from the Sahara were the fundamentalists of their time. Austere, rigorist, literalist, they decreed an unopposed Koranic order, slaughtering the population and destroying all the attributes of civilization. "The community's brilliance and easy living lasted thirty-five years. Then, those years vanished along with the people. As if awakened from some dream."[15] Ibn 'Ezra sought refuge in Castile, where he took to writing about those better times. This episode should serve as a reminder that the guest is also a hostage, even when he has obtained the right of residence. The descendents of Ibn Nagrila experienced the same slippery slope from guest to hostage, during a pogrom that ended in the slaughter of a great number of Jews, sparing not even the Naguid Yehūsaf, son of and successor to Ibn Nagrila in the post of prime minister.

Next, Nicholas Cusanus sees in a Christianity crossed with Platonism and Plotinism the religion that best corresponds to a religion of reason. He slips into his plea a surreptitious preference for Catholicism. This is what makes his text suspect in the eyes of a certain cohort of critics, notably Karl Jaspers.[16]

And finally, Ibn 'Arabī thinks that no religious sentiment or form of belief escapes the intuitive logic of God as expressed in the Koran. According to him, the religion concealed in every religion is *islām*, that is, the consenting of human contingency to the divine absolute, with the purpose of obtaining peace and salvation through submission. Humility is achieved after one undergoes the ordeal of humiliation through penitence.[17] It is nevertheless possible to subsume Islam as a particular religion, with its own rites, into the *islām* as analogue to natural religion.

Furthermore, we have the corrective to these traditional approaches by means of the radical Kantian one, which does not conserve his belief with the call for surpassing it. A reading of Kant accustoms us to a religious vision consistent with his cosmo-politics, oriented toward the goal of perpetual peace. His utopia ought to be ours, a means to organizing the republic where the three cultures, and more, could live and thrive together.

As for Christianity's relation to Judaism, the tradition of exclusion, from the evil of anti-Semitism all the way to genocide, has been seriously pondered and overcome. This achievement is the result of a long work of collective and individual soul-searching, involving psychic as well as intellectual and doctrinal revision. It is equally possible to overcome Islamophobia, a constituent element of European identity in the Middle Ages, with the ultimate episode of violence being the expulsion of the last Muslims from Western Europe, following the royal edict of 1609 handed down by the Spanish monarch.[18]

As for Muslims, they should go further in drawing inspiration from the advances within their own tradition in order to rediscover the conditions for overcoming their irredentism with regard to Christians, and more especially to Jews. It is the wedge issue of Israel that has spoiled relations among Jews on the one hand, and Muslims and Arabs on the other. We have seen how acknowledgment of Israel is the condition that leads to Jewish sovereignty.[19] And it is with sovereign Jews that the tradition of interfaith living can be restored, rectifying the former dissymmetry and inequality of the *dhimmi* status, which never really disappeared even during the heyday of Grenada's dream of religious cohabitation as witnessed by Ibn 'Ezra, a dream twice interrupted by massacres.

Muslims are now back in France and Europe once again. Islam emerged as a contemporary French and European issue as a result of the colonial experience, just as today's worsening situation is a post-colonial effect. I would like to revive an observation made by Tocqueville in 1847 in his parliamentary report,[20] where he denounced the two-pronged evil of France's authority in Algeria: It destroyed the local traditional education system that furnished, among others, the country's judiciary personnel, without replacing it by a pedagogy that would introduce the spirit of positive law; rather, the French made do with faithful but ignorant *cadis*. History vindicated Tocqueville, who believed that ignorance would eventually yield disastrous fanaticism.

In light of these remarks, I would say that the state's pedagogical duty would consist of making amends for this double failure, the colonial sin in the handling of the issue of Islam. This state should contribute to articulating Islam with the best of what its tradition has to offer, with the values inherited from the Enlightenment, which emphasize the primacy of reason in the constitution of an ethical, juridical, and political subject. What it would take is the widespread dissemination, both in the hearts and minds and in the school manuals, of the wealth of scholarship accumulated over the past two centuries on the topic of Islam. It would also take the

proper training of religious personnel in this double perspective: on
the one hand, an enlivened traditional science (oriented more toward exegesis and interpretation than toward theology and dog-
matic rehashing of old ideas); and on the other, a comparative
approach to religions in general, and an attitude toward history that
is receptive to the social sciences.

If all this can be accomplished, we will have participated in the
emergence of a post-Islamic subject, contemporary to the post-
Christian and post-Jewish counterpart. In the aftermath of this process, this getting beyond particular religions, the echoes of the first
religion will be heard, having become the final goal of the republic
of the three cultures. There will then be room for other expressions
from further afield, the nonmonotheistic cultural sphere, Japan,
China, India, and Africa. All of them, in their belief and nonbe-
lief, will thus collaborate to set in motion the cosmo-politics to
come, which in turn must be thought of in post-Western terms, in
the sense that it will constantly refine, correct, and rectify the Enlightenment's contribution, to free it from its shortcomings and ali-
bis, to push it beyond its own reductions, to release it from a system
mentality, rendering it more adaptable to different realities, subjecting it to the tension between the one and the many, as to that part
of the heart that "has its reasons that reason cannot know," to quote
Pascal.

It would seem that we have already entered into this historically
post-Western era, which, far from abolishing the Western legacy,
confirms it by correcting it, which strengthens its ambitious claim to
universality. Two political events precipitated this coming.

First, there was the end to apartheid led by the secular Nelson
Mandela, with the religious backing of Desmond Tutu, establishing
what Philippe-Joseph Salazar surmises to be the third foundation
reviving the concept of Republic, with the process triggered by the
release of Mandela in 1990, some two centuries after the American
independence in 1783 and the French Revolution of 1789.[21] One of
the contentious matters that all of white humanity stands accused
of, racism, in flagrant contradiction with the principles held dear by
this portion of the world, was settled once and for all with the for-
giveness by the victim during the highly dramatized scenes of acknowledgment of their crimes by those who had perpetrated them.

It is in this spirit that the social contract as conceived by Rousseau was founded anew. The association that protects all associates and their property was re-created through the sovereignty of solidarity that reframed the common good in which multiple components acknowledge one another in the diversity that makes up society as a whole.

The second event was the election of Barack Hussein Obama in November 2008, which placed at the summit of the world's most powerful nation a person bearing in his very name and body the three traumas that mark the century, that is to say, Africa, Islam, and urban segregation; or to put it differently, slavery, colonialism, and social inequality.[22] The political treatment put forward to cure these ills is once again far from resentment and a spirit of revenge. Rather, it involves a return to the principles of law and justice as they were traditionally conceived in the West but have been so rarely applied—in fact, as they were often flouted by the West itself, as it took up residence throughout the world. The power of fact has eclipsed the pertinence of ideas, and the powerful have been more concerned with preserving their hegemony, even when it means betraying the principles behind their own success.

It goes without saying that Islam has lagged behind when it comes to assimilating these new circumstances and entering into the post-Western, cosmo-political world that is finding a solid base in societies all over the world, one that could define the future, despite the fragility of a movement so susceptible to other forces ready to erase the gains made thus far, forces that know how to intensify the evil already corrupting our world.

**Appendix A:** THE VEIL UNVEILED: DIALOGUE
WITH CHRISTIAN JAMBET

*A.M.*: As a philosopher who deals in the concepts of Western tradition and Islamic thought, you are fluent in the conditions of both
rootedness and openness most likely to help us proceed to a fruitful
exegesis that will demonstrate the complexity of the veil issue. The
question is often addressed in the worst possible ways, starting with
the most basic ambivalence, contained in the phrase which appears
twice in the Koran, *min warā'i hijāb*, meaning "behind a veil" in its
literal translation.[1] The word *hijāb* or "veil" can be understood to
mean drapery, curtain, or partition separating two spaces. Never can
the word be taken in the reductive sense of a veil worn by women.

In the Koran, it is said: "When you ask the Prophet's wives for
something, ask them from behind a partition" (Koran 33:53). This
has to do with establishing a code of civility, with the partition, or
"veil," separating private from public space. The text here is explicit.
It cannot be read otherwise.

Again in the Koran, the same phrase recurs in a completely different context: "And it is not for any human being that Allah should
speak to him except by revelation or from behind a partition" (Koran
42:51).

Here, the expression is used in a metaphysical setting, after having
served in a more social circumstance. We move from a scene where the

partition, or veil, is staged as a civil instrument establishing separation between the sexes to one where the same veil intervenes to render visible the boundaries between human reception and divine message. With that in mind, we see that the same expression concerns on the one hand the management of male-female relations, in the erotic, social sense, based on a code of civility and modesty; and on the other hand, it involves the verbal link between God and humans.

Yet if we rely on the technique of *rasm al-qur'ān* (the graphics of the Koran), we note a difference in the transcription of the word *warā'i*, "behind": In 33:53, the word is written the same as it is today in newspapers, for instance, whereas in 42:51, the final hamza (*i*) is placed below the body of the letter *ya*, as if the reader were being invited to decipher the consonant and to vocalize it through the screen of the supplementary letter, this *ya* that serves as its support. This word (*warā'i*), which has the same meaning, which is pronounced the same way, is transcribed differently when used in the metaphysical setting, as if to signify a supplement, making of the unnecessary a necessity meant to remind the subject that he is in an exceptional situation when engaging with the Wholly Other.

*C.J.*: The distinction you have made between these two verses seems to me an absolutely central one. You have already provided the traditional explanation, or *tafsīr*, located in an extremely precise context. It raises the problem and provides an answer. The matter is less one of legality than "civility," as you so nicely put it. It deals with knowing how to enter the home of the Prophet of Islam, Muhammad, knowing which moral and physical precautions are to be taken. The second verse cited is about the approach of one who has been granted divine inspiration. There is no indication in the second verse as to who is actually receiving the inspiration. It is not necessarily the Prophet of Islam only, but could possibly be any inspired prophet, or a man with the gift of prophecy who is not himself a prophet.

But, assuming we are indeed dealing with the Prophet Muhammad here, a human being in the full sense, but gifted with exceptional powers, it is normal that he should possess a certain number of prerogatives. These entitlements distinguish him from other members of the community, and he benefits from certain procedures when being approached. Among these are the ones having to do with the veil. There is this matter of not being allowed to approach the spouses of the Prophet unless from behind a veil, though it remains unclear whether this veil is worn by the spouses or whether it implies simply a separation between two spaces, two locations, one sacred and the other profane.

*A.M.*: Based on how it appears in the verse, I would opt for spatial separation.

*C.J.*: If indeed it's about spatial separation, why was it ordained? Because the spouses of the Prophet pertain to the overall prophetic world. In this regard, for instance, we know how the prophet's daughter Fātima, spouse of 'Alī, came to be regarded as sacred, how the spouses were accorded special value, starting with Khadīja, the first, who is venerated in all Islam, to 'Ā'isha, an important link in the chain of transmission of several prophetic traditions. In contrast to this attitude, the Shiites curse 'Ā'isha but venerate those they call "the people of the prophetic house," that is, Muhammad, 'Alī, Fātima, Hassan, Husayn. For the Shiites, the "prophetic abode" extends to a still broader ensemble, to gradually include all the imams, and certain of their faithful, such as Salmān the Persian. Of course, all these notions, these spaces of veneration, if I may call them that, emerged during a time subsequent to Koranic revelation. But let us not forget that the Koranic vulgate we have today was also written subsequent to revelation, strictly speaking. To sum up, it is possible that such verses, by sketching out the notion of prophetic family or of the "prophetic house," underlie the future elaboration of the sanctification of feminine characters who, to varying degrees, were linked to the Prophet. In the Koranic text that you have cited, revelation suggests that the prophetic world, in a broader sense than the mere physical person of the Prophet himself, is surrounded by a kind of aura that creates a space that must be sanctified. Hence the ritual suggested here by the Koran, which organizes this spatial distinction. If we understand it in this way, the text is indeed normative, but not juridical, strictly speaking. It is not a matter of law, but rather of worship, a ritual form adapted to the space of the Prophet's home, to round out the only thing worthy of the name of worship, the standards of obedience of God in the order of practical life. It is interesting to find out why and how lawmakers were later able to make use of it.

*A.M.*: Because six verses further on, it is plainly stated that the wives of believers must wear modest dress: "Tell your wives and your daughters and the women of the believers to bring down over themselves part of their outer garments" (Koran 33:59). This is how I literally translate *yudnīna min jalābībihinna*, more often translated as "cover themselves with their veils," taking account of the exegetic tradition that unanimously perceives in this verse a prescription for women to wear the veil. The word *jalābīb* (plural of *jilbāb*) ought to be translated as tunic or overdress—it is the word from which derives the Moroccan *jellaba*. The recommendation to dress modestly has been interpreted as the requirement to veil. And this verse is consistent with the other verse that tradition invokes to unanimously legitimize the wearing of the veil. In this latter verse, it is recommended that women "wrap a portion of their headcovers over their chests" (*li-yuzribna bi-khumurihinna 'alā juyūbihinna*, Koran 24:31). Nowhere in either of these scriptural references does there appear the kind of veil that covers the head and hair, nor the traditional veils or the current one worn by women today.

*C.J.*: In verse 59, the injunction is no longer addressed to those who come to pay a visit to the Prophet, but to the Prophet himself. In effect, God commands him to tell his wives, then his daughters and finally the women of the believers (by a kind of progressive extension of the commandment's scope) to cover themselves in this way. It is the best way for them to be recognized for who they are, and not to be offended. It is a form of acknowledgment, of identification that has to do with appearance. It is thus paradoxical that this veiling is understood not as a way of covering up, but as a way of appearing, regulated by a dress code that involves modesty, ontological dignity (a way of distinguishing oneself from the unbelievers, or from women of less noble extraction), and the body of these women. As if their essence should appear, positively, in the clothing, and in the signs that keep at bay any immodest gaze or touch or word coming from an eventual outsider that would call into question these women's intrinsic purity.

*A.M.*: So, we're talking about a costume, along the lines of the Roman tunic, also a sign of noble, aristocratic distinction.

*C.J.*: Precisely. This isn't about a juridical prescription, but rather a moral one. A prescription that doesn't forbid or deny something, but rather gives rise to a positive mode of being, an ethos, which is a certain mode of appearance.

*A.M.*: Identification and recognition!

*C.J.*: Yes.

*A.M.*: But coming back to the expression "behind a partition" or veil, it's no coincidence that it has dominion over both a metaphysical scene and a more worldly one.

*C.J.*: All right, let's address the second verse that you mentioned earlier. First of all, we note that it is linked to the two others preceding it, and to another that follows. And they are of capital importance! Verse 49 deals with how the kingdoms of heaven and earth relate. It explains somehow one of the divine names that is present from the very first sūra of the Koran: the sovereign, the kingdom. Then comes the explanation of the infinite creative power of God. Next, the Koranic text makes a statement about revelation itself. In other words, how God speaks to Man. Régis Blachère, when translating this latter term into French, opts for "mortal," in its most classical meaning. This is not Man understood in the philosophical or naturalist sense, as a species, and even less "man" in the sense of masculine versus feminine. But Man is the living mortal, in his "creature-ness," which always translates into a radical ontological inferiority as compared to God. And here, we have three exemplary cases: inspiration or revelation, strictly speaking (*wahī*), then this "from behind a partition, or veil" and finally the messenger (*rasūl*), or he who brings the message of revelation (*risāla*). The third case is plain and simple: If there is a bearer of a message, there is no need for a veil, since the bearer is immediately in charge of the revelation that passes to the people for whom it is intended. Now, what about the other two cases? And here's something that is quite remarkable: Inspiration, or revelation, which has a broader meaning than "message," correlates to this "from behind the partition/veil." Both these cases concern all the modes of expression of the word God addresses to Man in the absence of living prophet-messengers. The veil, or "from behind the veil," symbolizes a generally common situation, that of the relationship between the divine Word, and the modes of apparition it provokes, and the human receptor. In other words, and even more profoundly, the relation between creator and creature. It is plain to see that the veil takes on a significance quite remote from the juridical domain: It designates the extremely complex relationship between God's transcendence and immanence. God is transcendent—he is always and forever behind a veil—and he is, in some way, immanent since his word abides in human receptacles prepared to receive it. This is what predisposes this particular verse to a considerable role in mystic and spiritual exegesis. And this is undoubtedly the most interesting angle of examination when it comes to the veiling issue. I believe we can concur on what I am about to suggest here: All juridical-political discussions surrounding the veil are fruitless unless we refer at some point to this word "veil" or "partition," and to this phrase "from behind a veil," in their far superior metaphysical sense, and without which all discussions amount to groping in the dark.

A.M.: The graphic supplement I pointed out earlier provides this verse (42:51) with the sign of this superior value. Moreover, an author such as Rāzī, the great exegete of the late twelfth century, in his monumental *tafsīr*, the *Mafātīh al-Ghayb* (The Keys to the Mystery), devotes several pages to it, and recalls the debate carried on by the *mu'tazila* (rationalist theologians of the early ninth century) over the fact that God speaks from behind a veil for a simple reason: When he speaks, he does so outside the letters and sounds of our custom. And when such a message comes into a human language, it must be mediated through an angel. Passage through the veil requires translation. In these precise conditions, for Koranic revelation itself, Rāzī reminds us that, in the famous debate over the created or uncreated Koran, we find we are armed with an argument that can be ascribed to the *mu'tazila* defending the notion of a created Koran. Passage through the veil requires an actualization of an eternal word into a contingent language: Thus, the unutterable and inaudible word of God can be uttered and heard through human intelligence.

*C.J.*: Once again, Fakhr al-Dīn al-Rāzī situated things at the right level. And this business of a created or uncreated Koran has numerous consequences, including in his *Commentary* on the Koran. As I understand it, there is a distinction to be made within the word of God itself, between what you call the unutterable and the inaudible (which is the reserve where this word is forever held, since it is infinite, the reserve of the uncreated essence of God), and the created Koran, or the created word in each prophetic utterance, which assumes in turn an exegetic interpretation. All this is to say that the meaning here of the word "veil" is nothing other than the sense of "apparent." The veil is that which is apparent (*zāhir*). And exegesis must then yield a plethora of hidden meanings in each prophecy. And all those meanings together are still incapable of exhausting the unutterable character of the word of God taken *in itself*: in what goes unrevealed, in what remains hidden. It is clear that all this takes us straight back to the veil par excellence: the Book. The Book is at once the Book itself as fact, the divine light, and the veil. An author I've studied quite a bit, Mollā Sadrā Shīrāzī (an Iranian author of the seventeenth century, who himself studied Rāzī's *Commentary* and made frequent use of it), does not comment on this verse explicitly. But with regard to the verse named "Of Light" (Koran 24:35), he says something very similar to what you have just pointed out about the Holy Book, when he says that this verse designates, in its spiritual signification, the Koran itself, the revealed Book. And the revealed Book clearly demonstrates this, as the light of both heaven and earth. It recapitulates in itself the light of all that exists, and, at the same time, it is by its very essence a veil, since many of its verses are obscure, and all its verses reveal and conceal at the same time. The Book therefore signifies both veiling and unveiling.

*A.M.*: And due to this phrase I keep referring to, the set of problems posed by veiling and unveiling (*kashf*) was to prove extremely meaningful to the Sufis. Here is a quote from one of the first Sufi masters, Abū Yazīd Bistāmī, who has God say: "If my servant makes me his chief occupation, I will put his appetite and delight in my invocation. I will lift the veil [and the word *ḥijāb* is used here] between him and me and will be the image forever before his eyes."[2] Thus, lifting the veil reveals the image of God, and not God himself. If we are to trust this saying, behind the veil we come face-to-face with God's image, but never with God!

*C.J.*: It's an amazing text where a multitude of references and correlations obviously come into play. When you say "from behind a veil," you never find divine essence itself but ever more veils, images, and manifestations—which is to say that the passage through the veil, the unveiling, resembles greatly what the Prophet himself experienced. It is said that during the Prophet's celestial journey through the heavens and up to the divine throne, he never came face-to-face with God, but within seventy, or according to others, 70,000 veils of light. That the veils were of light is worth noting: It proves that the veil is not a symbol of obscurity, a factor of obscurantism. In a certain sense, it is light itself that veils God during the Prophet's nocturnal journey. The veil is distance, and from this perspective, "behind the veil" is better understood. In French, at least, the word "behind" does not really indicate a spatial notion. Distance is not something that can be seen. Whereas in Arabic, it is indeed understood in this manner, and means "far behind the veil," with the veil creating an additional distance behind itself, if I may put it that way. So that when the Prophet accedes to God from behind 70,000 veils of light, it means he is experiencing a presence made of absence. Bistāmi, the mystic, had this same experience. God is an apparition, but in order to be so, he must disappear behind veils. It is ever thus: Appearing implies disappearing, for example, into an image that itself is nevertheless a mode of appearing. And if we are not able to intuit this, we transform the whole veiling issue into something almost vulgar.

*A.M.*: So this is about a kind of covering that is in fact a stripping bare!

*C.J.*: That's right. It is not possible to strip bare unless the thing is covered in the first place.

*A.M.*: So many masters of European art have experimented with this interplay of sheathing and laying bare, in both sacred and profane works. As for an example among the holy works, I'm thinking of an allegory of faith (1781) sculpted in Florence in the *cappella maggiore* of Santa Maria Maddalena dei Pazzi by the rococo artist Innocenzo Spinazzi, a native of Rome. When I saw that statue of a heavily veiled woman completely enveloped in fabric, I was struck by the resemblance between her accoutrement and the one worn by women I would cross paths with in the medina of Tunis, as they would strut in their clinging vernacular veils of white silk. They knew that beneath the veil there glimmered the possibility of flesh. It is as if Catholic iconography was inspired by Islamic anthropology in this staging of the mystery of faith, embodying within concealment itself a virtual truth disclosed. Such a process of revelation subjected to the tension between concealment and disclosure cannot avoid the nod to Eros that lies at the heart of religious subjects. It is hardly surprising, then, that this same operation underpins so many eminent profane representations in Western artistic traditions, here more overtly devoted to Eros, such as the pictorial meditation on the dressed and undressed as expressed by Goya's twin portraits of the same woman, one dressed, the other nude (*La Maja vestida*, 1799, and *La Maja desnuda*, 1800). And it is this pictorial memory that Marcel Duchamp seeks to divert in his playful, pseudo-esoteric work, *The Bride Stripped Bare by Her Bachelors, Even*.

*C.J.*: Yes, it's on that order. Like the veil of the Kaaba that both covers the holy place and manifests its presence.

*A.M.*: So there is indeed a connection between the metaphysical experience of the invisible and the veil as it pertains to the separation of the sexes and the reclusion of women. Here is another fragment from Bistāmi built around this very connection: "God's saints are hidden along with him behind the veil of intimacy. Like young girls kept at home, no one sees them, neither in this world or the next, except those few for whom the visit is licit. As for everyone else, they see them only in their veil. In truth, they see nothing but the veil."[3] It's rather surprising, isn't it, this merging of the spiritual position of the saint with the worldly position of women, as if the saint were God's spouse.

*C.J.*: It's no stranger than the feminine monastic tradition in Western Christendom, which makes the cloistered nuns brides of Christ, in the mystic sense of the term. God's saints (*awliyā'*) are those loved by God, closest to him, within his proximity. Indeed, proximity is the ultimate term of the spiritual experience, of the ascension of all the living toward their creator. And here they are, in the same position as women. It would seem to me that the text could go the other way as well. It could signify that the veiling of women turns them into *awliyā'*, saints or "beloved of God." They are protected by the veil because they are precious, because they are, in Bistāmi's words, in the "inner circle of angels," the rank of angels that are perpetually prostrate before the divine throne and worship in adoration. These women are not characterized by their inferior legal status, but by their amorous proximity to God. Here, we are relieved of several disparaging representations of women and, at least, of this absurd commonplace that says that all women share the same status in Islam, their status before the law. Here, the young woman is the symbol of a spiritual jewel.

*A.M.*: You mentioned cloistered nuns a moment ago. I'm thinking of Theresa of Avila in particular. Many passages of her spiritual biography (*My Life*) confirm what you have just said: she considers herself a bride of Christ. In the same Catholic tradition, John of the Cross addresses God in the feminine, in the place of femininity. And men who address God in this way, as do Bistāmi and John of the Cross, maintain the tension, the gap between gender and sex. Masculine by sex and feminine by desire, they are obliged to convert the gender of this desire from feminine to masculine, as in fragment 382 where Bistāmi converts into masculine the term *makhdurūn*, in principle used in the feminine, to designate female reclusion. Saintly women, on the other hand, are consistent in both sex and gender.

I return to Bistāmi with regard to his fascination with the feminine. Recall the two fragments concerning menstruation where he is at odds with the Koranic and prophetic sense that stigmatizes women's impurity.[4] Here is one of the two: "The condition of women is better than ours. Women are purified once a month, twice sometimes, for they bathe thoroughly after their menstruation. As for us, we are not even capable of such purity once in our lives." Thus does he inverse the prejudice by making impurity a condition for recovering purity, thereby ranking women before men, spiritually speaking, by virtue of this biological privilege and relegating men to their irreparable lack. These are some of the bold positions held by this master, who lived between the eighth and ninth centuries and who never left the high plateaus of his native Iran, near the Elburz Mountains, some three hundred kilometers north of Tehran. He was born in Bistām, the town that gave him his name, which, according to the twelfth-century geographer Qazwini, was famous for its apples, sought after even by the faraway court of the caliph of Baghdad.

*C.J.*: Yes, the climate there is particularly pleasant.

*A.M.*: Another fragment confirms this high praise for all things feminine. Allow me to read you this lovely anecdote in connection with the veil and women, and whose protagonist is again Bistāmi: "Umm 'Alī, a well-born young woman, decided to turn over to her husband Ahmad 10,000 dinars of her dowry on the condition that he take her to Abū Yazīd Bistāmi. He did so. She entered and sat before him, uncovering her face. Ahmad, her spouse, said to her: 'I have seen in you something strange—you have removed your veil before Abū Yazīd,' to which she responded: 'It's that when I look at him, I lose the energy of desire, and when I look at you, I regain it.' Upon leaving, Ahmad [Ibn Khuzhrawaya, also a Sufi, but of lesser importance] said to Abū Yazīd: 'What do you recommend to me?' and Bistāmi replied: 'Learn to be more chivalrous with your wife.'"[5]

*C.J.*: Yes, "Learn *futuwwa*," as he says. As for the spirit of chivalry, in this matter of desire, it would seem that what is at stake here is the relation of the saint, in this case Bistāmi, to purity and to the fact that he had purified his soul of all base passions.

*A.M.*: Can we evoke here what Lacan said about sexual nonrelations? It's known that Lacan elaborated his theory based particularly on the writings of mystics.

*C.J.*: Let us posit that the husband is separated because he is experiencing desire. He is necessarily bound to a nonrelation, as materialized by the veil. In the presence of the saint, the man of God,

Bistāmi, the woman can unveil. First of all, since there is no question of a sexual relation here either. But especially because the visit
to this man in itself signifies a disclosure, an unveiling, and she has
just learned and acknowledged this. She is thus freed from a veil that
has become useless, for something has happened: the apparition
within her, on her face, of a truth that Bistāmi never ceases to repeat
in a most paradoxical fashion, when he says: "Glory be to me." In a
certain way, the woman says "Glory be to me," and she shows within
her a divine epiphany. This is how I understand it; otherwise, why
would this anecdote be reported so often *in this form*? Why would
this woman perform such a paradoxical act before her spouse?

Getting back to impurity, I am struck, in the prophetic traditions
devoted to impurity, by the Prophet's obsession to prevent and elim-
inate it, or if I dare say, to "exorcise" it. And I mean all forms of impurity here. He lives in the constant dread of dying impure, something
which is clearly present in certain of his prayers. Everything points
toward it! It could be that the Koran bears testimony, when Muhammad receives the revelations about menstruation and other events on
this order, to this anxiety of the male before that most basic impurity of the sexual body, to the Prophet's own obsession. So much so
that one might wonder whether, prior to the revelation episodes, he
had not perhaps inherited a certain number of concerns very close to
the Manichaean or ascetic forms typical of Eastern Christianity.

*A.M.*: Could you say a little more about that proximity?

*C.J.*: I am struck by the fact that prophetic traditions—having to do
with menstrual blood, excrement, anything that is base and impure
in the body—or the prayers of the Prophet Muhammad that seem
to obsess over the possibility that he could die impure in his sleep,
translate a concern that we find in Manichaeism and in certain
forms of Judeo-Christian asceticism, to reduce all the body's areas of
darkness. This resonates with the perception that Suhrawardī's disciples had of the veil, around the turn of the twelfth century. They
maintain that the veil is the body itself, since it is dark and unfath-
omable. Everything having to do with purification of the body, everything we find in the Koran in this regard, takes on a significance that
goes far beyond some moral precepts. We are to preserve the salva-

tion of the light of the soul from everything coming from the obscure, murky body. This is not a juridical matter whatsoever, but an ontological one. The body is, on the one hand, the place where divine light makes its appearance, but on the other, via all that is material and lowly (and that signifies, in this case, the dangerous productions of the female body or the human body in general), it symbolizes a mortal material essence. One must be delivered of it, and unveiling implies first and foremost freeing oneself of the perishable condition of the dark body. It's quite interesting, after all, that Suhrawardī's disciples translated the word *barzakh*, which signifies "in between," and also "isthmus," and which has taken on many meanings of veiling in an even more radical manner. For them, *barzakh* is "the substance of night and death," the body that veils the prophetic soul from itself, separating us from ourselves and from divine light. The concern over impurity in that sense has nothing to do with superstition. It doesn't consist in saying: "Beware, for if you have any intimacy during the woman's menstruation, or if you are not careful about your own bodily secretions and excretions, you will be impure and will thus be rejected." This is not it. Rather, in this attention devoted to the body, to bodily materials, the faithful acknowledge the unfortunately double essence of human creatures. On the one hand, light, on the other, darkness. The veil placed on the body does nothing more than to reveal the body itself as veil. This is why what interests all the Muslim authors mentioned here is not the veil but the unveiling, the disclosure, which is to say, liberation.

*A.M.*: In all, then, veils of any kind imply *kashf*, unveiling or disclosure. The term itself is ambivalent, belonging to both an erotic vocabulary and the more technical lexicon of the mystics. The first treatise of Sufism in Persian was written by Hujwīrī in the eleventh century and was titled *Kashf al Mahjūb*,[6] which literally means "uncover what is veiled," and it is indeed a call to lift the veil, to analyze the experience that leads to revealing what is concealed, in other words, to the revelation of mysteries, the visibility of the Invisible. The word *mahjūb*, "veiled," is based on the same root as *hijāb*, "veil," a word that has become familiar to Westerners, the French in particular, since the media have ushered it into common usage, albeit through the wrong door.

The word *kashf* is also used in everyday language with regard to
the voyeur when his field of vision extends to a private space protected by the introverted architecture of houses turned in upon an
interior courtyard. When I was a child, my grandfather (who was a
pious man), as soon as he would see a male on the terrace of the
house next to ours, he would shout, "Watch out for *kashf*!" The use
of this word in such a circumstance is consistent with the Koranic
recommendation that we scrutinized earlier, the one that requires
that private space in the Prophet's house be kept separate "behind a
veil" (33:53), a requirement that eventually brought about the concept of the Muslim home closed upon itself, a protected space
around a patio, cut off from the public network and unavailable to
the outsider's eye. Thus, two words go hand in hand, even anthropo-
logically: *kashf* and *hijāb*, both of which are used in both the sexual
and metaphysical applications. It is therefore in the words themselves that the erotic energy of Muslim mysticism is revealed.

*C.J.*: You've given an accurate account of the separation between the
home and public space. The home is a place of concealment, but in a
very powerful sense. The concealed is the space of secrecy or privacy,
but also of the real. It should not be thought of as a kind of cloister-
ing, but rather a protection of what is most important. As for the
erotic side of Muslim mysticism, you are quite right to emphasize
this.

*A.M.*: And it is Bistāmi who exploits this ambivalence by revealing
the erotic intimacy that links the initiate to God behind the veil.[7]

*C.J.*: We could reach all the way back to the pre-Islamic odes to
which Islam is greatly indebted in that regard. The dialectic of love
presupposes a veil of some kind. With 'Attar, for instance, the old
man walking down an alleyway falls in love with a young lady that
he saw for only a split second, and behind a veil. This assumes that
the cause of love is precisely that which is veiled. As for unveiling
itself, you mentioned Hujwīrī, but the title will be reprised constantly: "the disclosure of hidden things." It's more than a title, it's a
whole program! There's a need for the mind, for spiritual experience,
to go beyond appearances, or to restore appearance to its true status,

to make it a place of apparition. To do this, one must show what it is that appears in the apparent, what we call the hidden. Unveiling, or disclosure, is the term that will become technical, standard, to describe the work of philosophers, the experience of poets, of lovers, and of mystics. In short, all cultural and intellectual experiences, even sentimental and affective ones, in the Muslim world. This is the dialectic of veiling and unveiling.

A.M.: The veil is a reality and a metaphor that calls for a stripping away, and acts at both the sexual and metaphysical levels. This double occurrence of *kashf* is confirmed by a remark made by Ibn 'Arabī (1165–1240), whom you have read assiduously, under the guidance of Henry Corbin, who produced a memorable monograph of this great Sufi that tradition has named "the greatest master," *ash-Shaykh al-Akbar*.[8] I'm referring to the first poem in his collection *Tarjumān al-Ashwāq*, translated into French under the title *L'Interprète des desires*,[9] the interpreter of desires. Ibn 'Arabī stages Balqīs, the queen of Sheba, as she is theatrically narrated in the Koran (27:28–44). Indeed, she is involved in one of the most beautiful scenes of the Holy Book. To test her ability to judge false appearances, Solomon invites her to enter the palace. Mistaking the crystal flooring for a pool of water, she lifts her skirts, uncovering her shins to wade through. And it is the verb *k.sh.f.* (the root of the word *kashf*) that is used. Subjected to a trick test, she proceeds to uncover herself in an erotic way. Believing that she sees in the solid floor a liquid, she bares her legs for fear of getting her garment wet. And Ibn 'Arabī, in one of his more masterful moves, has this story resonate with another eschatological verse that uses the same expression: *Kashf as-Sāq*, "uncovering the leg" (Koran 68:42)—translated by Blachère into French as "le jour où l'on découvrira le danger," or "the day danger will be discovered," while the Arabic text reads: "the day the leg [shin] will be discovered," a gesture suggesting disorder in the rush provoked by the upheaval of the Apocalypse. Through this association, Ibn 'Arabī is anchoring ever more solidly in scripture the complicity between the sexual and the metaphysical.

C.J.: We can also imagine that Ibn 'Arabī is thinking of one of the prophetic prerogatives of Judgment Day, when he attributes it to this woman, and that is not only to preside over the sorting of souls into "people of the right" and "people of the left," the just and the impious, but also to unveil effective reality as it will be and as it is. The Prophet's prerogative is to see things as they really are. In this interplay with the queen of Sheba, as with the day of danger, the veils are lifted. All semblance vanishes and the real is laid bare. There is immense resonance with all that in Ibn 'Arabī. The unveiling effected by the spiritual is none other than that effected by prophetic power. In this story and in the interpretative connections made by Ibn 'Arabī, we perhaps find all these resonances. The queen of Sheba, following an amusing misapprehension, a kind of trompe l'oeil, achieves an unveiling, an uncovering that has an eschatological and prophetic meaning, and is none other than the act that Ibn 'Arabī is accomplishing.

*A.M.*: In this poetry collection, we witness the stages and processes of unveiling, of disclosure, in the play of consonance and mirroring between human passion and mad love (whose perfect, though not exclusive, model remains *Majnūn Laylā*—the Madman and Layla, or the Man Who Was Mad over Layla) and divine love, experienced in the multitude of forms assumed by the One. Through the experience of diverse love figures, it is the idea of the One that is unveiled. This diversity is illustrated by the numerous women's names and couples madly in love, the best known of profane literature, meant to serve as exemplars for divine love. The multiplicity of love figures is but the reflection of the many forms of belief: To the Byzantine icon, to the queen of Sheba, to the lovers from Arabia, Hind, Layla, Maya, Buthayna, to all of them corresponds the multiplicity of forms of belief, represented in the single space of revealed scripture, the four Books: the Gospels, the Psalms, the Torah, and the Koran, whose texts help orient spiritual meditation. And since each woman's name evoked is but the translation of the Lady who provides inspiration, Nizām (*Harmonia*), the young Persian woman encountered in Mecca, it is also proper to interpret in each form of belief the revelation of the Wholly Other. The unveiling consists therefore of penetrating the veils of the many to recover the truth of the One.

*C.J.*: Which is to say that those who are veiled, in the pejorative sense, are those who do not perceive this divine epiphany in the four divine Books.

*A.M.*: Which is another way of saying we would include among those veiled ones the legal experts and anyone who gives precedence to the politico-juridical dimension of the Koran. In short, those who reduce the infinite of the Koran to the paucity and misery of prescriptive measures that have been totally surpassed by human evolution.

*C.J.*: Let me remind you that the expression "the veiled ones" (*al-Mahjūbūn*) is used with contempt by spiritual persons or mystic philosophers. But the most satisfying French translation is "the ignorant or unenlightened ones." Henry Corbin translates it as *les ignorantins*. We are not talking about ordinary ignorance here, for the word refers to those whose spiritual sense has been veiled. And in this case, the veil belongs to whoever believes in the veil, who thinks literally that, to please God, one need only see to it that women are veiled, without understanding what the veil means. They are the jurists, the literalist theologians and all their followers.

*A.M.*: And all the troublemaking ideologues of today!

*C.J.*: They are the upholders of the veil, one might say, but of a veil that offends them at the same time. Which is why the truly faithful are those who unveil the meaning of the word "veil" and who understand the importance of this theology of the veil, this mystic side of the veil, which you have just explained. Only then can one properly evaluate, if need be, the various juridical discourses.

*A.M.*: Given what is currently going on with regard to the veil, we can assume that the whole point has been degraded. Today's situation is the perfect illustration of a lack of understanding among non-Muslims, and an amnesia among Muslims.

*C.J.*: The amnesia among, let's say, a certain number of Muslims, those who have an interest in forgetting, those who absolutely insist on turning the veil crisis into a problem of *fatwa*, of juridical councils. It is no less alarming that those who contest them are also grounded in a legislative terrain. Because this legislative terrain—and I'm not taking sides on the issue as to whether or not legislation ought to be involved; that's not my point—is a minefield. We have cited Ibn ʿArabī, Rāzī, Bistāmī, Suhrawardī, a sum of references that prove that the genuine intellectual world of Islam, including the theological sphere, cannot be reduced to the juridical terrain. And on the basis of this immense universe of exegesis, we should justly gauge the issue as to whether, today, the education of Muslims by Muslims should take the form of a juridical discussion, or whether it should raise the understanding of the whole veil phenomenon to an infinitely richer degree. In this matter, it is the moral horizon we should be aiming for. For finally, the verse, to come back to it for the last time, that advises modesty for women, girls, and believers, implies a scope of meaning that cannot be reduced to a juridical order. This moral prescription has extremely serious resonances in that it goes together with what you just now referred to as the *erotic*. It means that the question of desire, of love, is a matter to be taken absolutely seriously.

*A.M.*: The *kashf*, erotically speaking, is the laying bare of the body. And metaphysically, it is the laying bare of mysteries, in other words, revelation, through entering into the world of the Invisible and of Absence.

*C.J.*: What is unfortunate about Western culture in its dealings with Islam, either at home or abroad, is that no one is really asking the right questions about the veil or unveiling, since the body has become anything but a subject of metaphysical questioning, reduced as it is to medical and legal issues. Natural law in the West, which in so many other instances has been a good thing for us, has done us the disservice of preventing us from conceiving of the body for what it really is, that wholly enigmatic apparition of a place of desire, and therefore a place of danger, as Ibn ʿArabī said when referring to the "day of danger," and consequently as a place infinitely different from all other celestial or terrestrial bodies, something that, in its very flesh, is visited by the spirit. That is something our thinkers have perhaps forgotten, for there also exists a Western amnesia that favors, alas, the worst misunderstandings, often resulting in confrontation.

*A.M.*: Our conversation, though technical at times, has been wide ranging, and we've made some fairly bold connections, but I think we are in complete agreement on this: an unqualified refusal of the veil as a sign of inferior legal status for women, a notion whose proliferation we are both striving to contain. Where the French context is concerned, I would opt for a clear, simple law that could be summed up in one sentence, so that it doesn't in turn give way to all kinds of casuistic discussion: "It is formally forbidden to wear conspicuously religious signs at school." Nothing more, nothing less. Once this precondition has been agreed upon, we can have the kind of discussion we have had today, benefiting from the enormous freedom and means that our times allow, authorizing us to revisit the crucial ideas of bygone eras, and at times subverting them by releasing them from the constraints of belief, for we are enjoying the immense privilege of speaking and writing in the absence of persecution, as Leo Strauss once put it.

*C.J.*: I am definitely with you on that point. What is so awful about reducing things to their legal aspect—and that was my point a moment ago—is that, in France, we grant overriding status to certain juridical discourses born in the lands of Islam in our dialogue or thought processes regarding what we call, inappropriately, by the way, "integration." This decision has had catastrophic consequences, for the juridical inferiority of women, whether it pertains to their status as witnesses or to the price of blood—murder of a woman is considered a lesser crime—or to matters of inheritance, all these things are the inventions of legal experts and belong to one discourse among others, that of jurisprudence, and as such is perfectly respectable, but cannot and should not lay claim to the whole spectrum of discussion. If we situate ourselves exclusively in this territory of what is legal and what is not, we will have nothing to say in response to the juridical status of inferiority for women, for it will come down to an argument over one law against another. But the "law" to which another law responds is not an absolute, but a series of statements.

*A.M.*: What we simply cannot allow to stand is the attitude of "the ignorant ones," these people who are in thrall to the veil, those who would impose historically specific discourses and jurisprudential constructions as representing the very essence of Islam. We should not yield an inch to the juridical discourse. To do so would amount to admitting that the growing role of Islam in Western culture will represent something regressive, a fundamentally obscurantist stance, one that aims to weaken what we generally call the reign of freedom.

*C.J.*: When fundamentalists dish out the Koranic text outside its context, and in its bare essentials, we are often confronted with idiotic, and at times dreadful, injunctions. We will not accept that, in the name of Islam, the worst should prevail. I feel it is crucial that the approach of the philosopher and the poet should be to absorb the Koran as a fact that has already been overwhelmed by countless layers of tradition. In this way, we will confine what is outmoded in Koranic law to the category of perishables, even though this is the whole cloth out of which our opponents have fashioned the very banners of Islam. I believe that it is by means of exercises like the one in which we have taken part today that we shall succeed in this labor of absorption, selection, and containment.

## Appendix B: OBAMA IN CAIRO

The speech delivered on June 4, 2009, at the University of Cairo by President Obama is first of all immensely appropriate and timely. It lays down the principles for alleviating the turbulent relations between Islam and the West. It takes on the stereotypes that rule out and demonize Islam, and does so in the name of an ethics of responsibility. And it demands in return that Islam do the same with its reductive vision of the West, and America in particular. The ethics of responsibility requires reciprocity.

This call to revise one's representations to restore the other's dignity is the condition that establishes genuine respect. By refreshing the representation of Islam in the Western mind, Obama is attempting a form of integration that puts an end to the sense of exclusion that currently affects Muslims. Louis Massignon traced the archaeology of that exclusion from the early beginnings: He returns to the figure of the first outcast, Ishmael, son of the servant Hagar, child of an illicit union with Abraham. According to the myth, Mohammedan lineage begins with Ishmael. In fact, in medieval times, Jews called Muslims variously Hagarites or Ishmaelites. With this exclusion of Islam by Judeo-Christians, Muslims experienced one of their narcissistic wounds. This wound was assumed and healed by interior discipline so long as Muslims, and Arabs in particular, could lean on their aristocratic values, imbued by a spirit of chivalry and laws of hospitality that granted guest status to the outsider, even when the latter behaved as an aggressor or invader.

This is how the figure of Emir Abd el-Kader is identified, he who despite defeat at the hands of the French never felt resentment toward them. These aristocratic values remained active, even during the colonial era. It illuminated the souls of peoples reduced to misery and frustration. It was only in the late 1920s, with the emergence of the semiliterate on the political scene of Islamic societies, that an ethics of resentment started to take hold, whereby the zealot of Islam reacted to Western domination. Refusing exclusion, which he experienced as a humiliation, he decided to take the path of violence (even when it turned criminal) as a response to his oppressor. This is the breeding ground that proved so welcoming to the fundamentalist seed, which then germinated, grew, and thrived. In the shadow of this new foliage sprang up the Muslim Brotherhood, some of whom were to become followers of al-Qā'ida.

Obama's integrating discourse seeks to free Islam from the figure of resentment that is thriving in al-Qā'ida's sphere of influence. The integration of Islam starts with the acknowledgment of the debt that civilization owes this culture. Obama does this clearly, simply, naming specific instances. In a few summary sentences, he delivers to the public at large what is deposited in the historical archive. Not only does he situate in our joint time frame Muslim achievements in astronomy, mathematics, and medicine, he also refers to their contributions to art and beauty through architecture and calligraphy, creating spaces conducive to contemplation and meditation.

Most important, however, he is foregrounding the Islamic reference, opening it up and getting it back into circulation as a material capable of enriching human experience. To this end, he makes two explicit references to the Koran, choosing verses that can guide not only Muslims but all humanity. It is thus as a non-Muslim, as an avowed Christian, that he is making use of the Koranic reference. Verse 70 of sūra 33 (there is another occurrence in 9:9): "O you who have believed, fear God and speak the truth." (This is the American translation currently in use, but *sadīd* means rather "just, right, that which aims at its objective." "Effective" might be the closest meaning. Jacques Berque translates the term into French as "adequate," which signifies appropriateness. Another frequently used translation is "adequate justice," instead of "truth.") And with this quote, Obama indeed lives up to the injunction to speak the truth, as he continues his speech before the Cairo audience. For in it, he speaks the truth, his aim is sure, his words are right, effective, and appropriate. He does not reserve his innermost thoughts to what gets confided only behind closed doors, but speaks out in such a way as to be heard far and wide. He is respecting the rule he set for himself in his speech on race in America, when he was running for president, and responding to the hateful statements of his pastor, Reverend Wright, a man steeped in resentment. Political discourse will henceforward be based upon true speech that will not seek to elude the issues, but will define them before attempting to offer solutions.

It is in this spirit that Obama lays out the first of six points he will develop, the one having to do with the deadly violence perpetrated by Islamist extremists. Note that he distances himself from the neo-conservative discourse adopted by G. W. Bush by refraining from calling them "terrorists" or "Islamofascists." At this stage, he quotes the Koran once again, speaking to those who condone the acts of their fellow Muslims who slaughter innocents in the name of God, justifying this criminal act as a pious work that will grant them the absolution of martyrdom, where suicide attacks are concerned. Obama's condemnation of these acts of murder is based upon the radical pronouncement in the Koran with regard to homicide: "Whoever killed a human being, except as punishment for murder or other villainy in the land, shall be deemed as though he had killed all mankind; and that whoever saved a human life shall be deemed as though he had saved all mankind." By referring to this scriptural reference, the American president castigates violent elements among Muslims, those acting out of resentment. Thanks to this Koranic material, he casts out those Muslims who would point to exclusion and oppression endured by Muslims in the past to justify their present destructive actions.

Furthermore, in the unfolding of his argument, President Obama uses two other references drawn from Holy Scripture to bring Islam into the frame of joint lived experience that we so sorely need today. He recalls that period when Islam was at the height of its grandeur, the splendor of Baghdad and Cordova, when three religious communities lived together and thrived. This past glory should be conducive to making Islam a present and future partner. Obama links Islam to the project of tomorrow's community, one that could bring people together while preserving their difference and diversity. This future community is also inspired by the Latin formula stamped on the Great Seal of the United States and quoted by Obama: *E pluribus unum* (Out of many, one), an imperial Roman principle, reoriented by Catholic universalism, and which we in turn can adopt for the globalization we are in the process of achieving in this new century.

The first of the references used by Obama to exemplify his point comes from the *Mi'rāj*, the story that tells of the Ascension of the Prophet, where it is said that Muhammad prayed in the heavens with Jesus and Moses. Since the celestial traveler left from Jerusalem, Obama cites this unifying scene to elevate it as a symbol of the thrice holy city, one of whose vocations is to be shared among Jews, Christians, and Muslims. In short, as Nicholas of Cusa suggests, Jerusalem would become the capital of universal religion tucked into the folds of particular religions. It is this vision—which is shared by Kant and the Enlightenment thinkers—that Obama is proposing as he addresses the world from his podium in Cairo, according to the discursive modalities that restore the persuasive potential of oration in politics.

Finally, the American president lends his last reference a conclusive function by placing the Muslim holy book at the same level as the Talmud and the Bible, thereby granting ethical credit to the Koran with respect to Judeo-Christian scripture. Such an act reaffirms the will to coexistence among Jews, Christians, and Muslims in respect and mutual recognition, to put an end to mutual denial and exclusion that evildoers feed upon and exploit to spread their sinister message. Thus, alongside the Talmud and the Bible, the Koran is taken up once again by Obama when he quotes 49:13: "O mankind, indeed We have created you from male and female and made you peoples and tribes that you may know one another." This Koranic notion of *ta'āruf*, which recommends recognition by comingling, converges toward the same horizon of peace mapped out in certain citations from the Talmud and the Bible.

All the remaining points made by the Cairo speech demonstrate that Obama has neither concealed nor conceded anything essential. Still, the causes of friction and misunderstanding are stated with an elegance that does leave certain things implicit, so as not to appear to be lecturing his public. Though many will find fault with this speech for any number of reasons, I will not linger on what he said regarding Iran, democracy, religious freedom, or women's rights. I turn my gaze instead toward the sequence devoted to the conflict in the Holy Land.

Obama urges Muslims and Arabs to acknowledge Israel, inviting them to assimilate the objective reasons that legitimize the existence of a state for the Jews, as a radical remedy for millennia of mistreatment and prejudice that culminated in the horror of the Holocaust. While emphasizing this yet unfulfilled recognition among Muslims, and unqualifiedly condemning Holocaust denial, he does not allow all that to overshadow the tragic consequences of the creation of Israel, that is to say, the suffering of the Palestinian people, who are oppressed and despoiled at every turn. He urges these same Palestinians, however, to forswear violence, which only leads to deadlock. He evokes the success of those who have suffered as much as they have: blacks, from South African apartheid to the segregated southern United States. By means of this appropriate analogy, he suggests that Nelson Mandela and Martin Luther King Jr. were able to break the deadlock by means other than deadly confrontation against a repressive, disproportionately powerful apparatus.

There were many the world over who took issue with this speech, finding it utopian, mollifying, irenic, apolitical. Some felt it was purely rhetorical, and are waiting for these words to translate into acts. I think such critiques are missing the point, for what matters in this speech are the principles it has laid down. Its author is well aware that the political path that is supposed to implement these principles is a rough one, requiring "perseverance and patience," as he himself put it. But for us, the letter of the principle is of major importance, for it kindles the light that will show the way to action. It matters little that, for the moment, the acts dishonor the principles. Yes, we have fallen short of the goal, but this is only a temporary setback proving that the acts desired are only deferred. Mishaps do not alter what is essential. And clearly defined principles will shape acts, correct them, and project them into a future that will make way for their coming.

# Notes

PROLOGUE: RELIGION AND VIOLENCE

1. *La Maladie de l'Islam* (Paris: Seuil, 2002); *Face à l'Islam* (Paris: Textuel, 2004); *Contre-prêches* (Paris: Seuil, 2006); *Sortir de la malédiction* (Paris: Seuil, 2008). Available in English: *The Malady of Islam* (New York: Basic Books, 2003).

2. Ou-Yang Hsui, *Hsin T'ang Shu*, trans. Isaac Mason as "The Mohammedans of China cited by Robert G. Hoyland in *Seeing Islam as Others Saw It* (Princeton, NJ: Darwin Press, 1997), 250–51.

1. THE KORAN AS MYTH

1. Dante, *De Vulgari Eloquentia*, trans. Steven Botterill (Cambridge: Cambridge University Press, 1996).

2. As observed by Ibn al-Haytham in his *Manāzir/De Optica*, in the eleventh century; see Kamāl ad-Dīn Abā 'l-Hasan al-Fārisī, *Kitāb tanqīh al-Manāzir li-dhawīy al-abçār wa 'l-baçā'ir*, ed. Mustafā al-Hijāzī (Cairo:Mustafā al-Hijāzī 1984), I: 261. In English: *The Optics of Ibn al-Haytham, Books I–III: On Direct Vision, Books 1–3*, trans. A. I. Sabra (London: Warburg Institute, 1989).

3. *Rasā'il Ikhwān as-Safā' wa Khillān al Wafā* (Beirut: Dār Sādir, 1957), 1: 219–25.

4. Among the numerous treatises on this issue, see Al-Bāqillānī, *I'jāz al-Qur'ān* (Cairo: Dār al-Ma'ārif, 1963).

5. Abū 'l-Alā' al-Ma'arrī, *Risālat al-Ghufrān* (Cairo: 'A'isha 'Abd ar-Rahmān, 1969).

6. Spinoza, *Theological-Political Treatise,* ed. Jonathan Israel and Michael Silverthorne (Cambridge: Cambridge University Press, 2007).

7. Among the dozens of popular editions that crowd bookstores and stalls, I cite a finer edition, which brings together *Tafsīr al-'Az'īm* by Ibn al-Kathīr in one volume of over two thousand pages in fine print (Beirut: Dār Ibn Hazm, 2000).

8. Tabarī, *Jāmi' al-Bayān fi Ta'wīl al Qur'ān,* 15 vols. (Beirut: Sidqī Jamīl al-'Attār, 1999).

9. Zamakhsharī, *Al-Khashshāf,* 4 vols. (Cairo: M.S. Qamhāwī, 1972); Fakhr ad-Dīn Rāzī, *Mafātīh al-Ghayb,* 32 books in 16 vols. (Beirut: n.p., 1990).

10. Anecdote told by Michel Chodkiewicz in *Le Sceau des Saints. Prophétie et sainteté dans la doctrine d'Ibn Arabī* (Paris: Gallimard, 1986), 106–7.

11. Ibn 'Arabī, *Tarjumān al-Ashwāq,* trans. Reynold A. Nicholson (London: Theosophical Publishing House, 1911).

12. François Déroche, *Manuel de codicologie des manuscrits en écriture arabe* (Paris: BNF, 2000).

13. Christoph Luxenberg, *Die Syro-aramäische Lesart des Koran. Ein Beitrag zur Entschlüsselung der Koransprache* (Berlin: Das Arabische Buch, 2000).

14. Alfred-Louis de Prémare, *Les Fondations de l'Islam. Entre écriture et histoire* (Paris: Seuil, 2002); Alfred-Louis de Prémare, *Aux origines du Coran. Questions d'hier, approches d'aujourd'hui* (Paris: Téraèdre, 2004).

## 2. THE CLASH OF INTERPRETATIONS

1. The *jizya* is a tax imposed on the *dhimmi,* or minority, protected by the Islamic authority.

2. Jan Assmann, *Le Prix du monothéisme* (Paris: Aubier, 2007).

3. Which I have already begun in "Le partage," *Dédale* 3–4, *Multiple Jérusalem* (Spring 1996): 16.

4. Jacques Berque, *Le Coran. Essai de traduction* (Paris: Albin Michel, 2002), 202.

5. Israeli-American professor Amitai Etzioni, director of the Institute for Communitarian Policy Studies at George Washington University.

6. President of the Islamic Republic of Iran from 2001 to 2005.

7. *Allah* is the word for God in Arabic, quite simply. To say "Allah" in French or English does not involve any additional meaning.

8. Alfonso X el Sabio, *Cantigas de Santa Maria*, four illustrated codices of illuminations, two conserved at Escurial, the third in Madrid, the fourth in Florence.

9. Louis Massignon, "La *Futuwwa*" or "Pacte d'honneur artisanal entre les travailleurs musulmans du Moyen Âge," in *Écrits mémorables* (Paris: Robert Laffont, 2009), 1: 613–39.

10. Esther W. Goodman, "Samuel Halevi Abulafia's Synagogue (El Transito) in Toledo," *Jewish Art* 18 (1992): 58–69.

11. She lived for about two years in Constantinople, modern Istanbul (1717–18). See Lady Mary Wortley Montagu, *The Complete Letters of Lady Mary Wortley Montagu*, 3 vols., ed. Robert Halsband (Oxford: Clarendon Press, 1966–67).

12. She spent three weeks at the residence of the Effendi of Belgrade during her travels to Istanbul.

13. Term often translated as "polytheist," used in Islam to designate an idolater, he who in his worship associates some other minor deity with the One God. The Trinity gets assimilated into this "associationist" operation.

14. Jean Damascène, *Ecrits sur l'Islam* (Paris: Editions du Cerf, 1992), 218–19. In English, *The Fathers of the Church* (Washington, D.C.: Catholic University of America Press), 37: 153–60 ; "St. John of Damascus's Critique of Islam," Orthodox Christian Information Center, 2006, http://orthodoxinfo.com/general/stjohn_islam.aspx.

15. Ibn 'Arabī, *Tarjumān al-Ashwāq*, trans. Reynold A. Nicholson (1911, repr. London: Theosophical Publishing House, 1978), 70. (Translator's note: In the original French, Meddeb provides his own translation, which he says was inspired by the poetics of Mallarmé that helped him bring this medieval poem to a contemporary audience.)

160 *Notes to pages 23–34*

16. As if in echo of a fragment by Heraclitus: "The sun is new every day." Charles Kahn, *The Art and Thought of Heraclitus: An Edition of the Fragments with Translation and Commentary* (Cambridge: Cambridge University Press, 1979).

17. Ezra Pound, *ABC of Reading* (London: G. Routledge, 1934).

18. Ibn 'Arabī, *Tanazzul al-Amlāk fī Harakāt al-Aflāk*, ed. Nawāf al-Jarrāh (Beirut: Dār Sadar, 2003), 22.

19. Michel Chodkiewicz elucidates this in his lovely book, *Le Sceau des saints* (Paris: Gallimard, 1986).

20. Ibn 'Arabī, *Al-Futūhāt al-Makkiyya*, vol. 2 (Cairo: N.p, n.d.), 262.

21. "There is not upon those who believe and do righteousness any blame concerning what they have eaten in the past if they now fear Allah and believe and do righteous deeds [*'amilū aç-çālihāt*]" (Koran 5:93). This verse comes on the heels of two others that recommend avoiding wine.

22. This Koranic reminiscence, 6:74–79, prompts us to note that Maimonides is inspired by Islamic Scripture.

23. Mūsa Ibn Maymūn (Arab name for Maimonides), *Dalālat al-Hā'irīn* (Cairo: Husayn Atāy, n.d.), 157, 580–91. In English, *The Guide of the Perplexed*, trans. Shlomo Pines, intro. Leo Strauss (Chicago: University of Chicago Press, 1974).

24. Michel Cuypers, *Le Festin. Une lecture de la sourate "Al-Mā'ida"* (Paris: Lethielleux, 2007).

25. Whose principle criterion is that of "doing righteousness" (*'amala çālihān*), of the verse analyzed earlier (5:69).

26. This article first appeared in *Politique Etrangère* 2 (May 1949): 139–152, and was reprinted in an issue of the journal *Ethnies* devoted to Levi-Strauss and the Nambikwara: Claude Levi-Strauss, "La politique étrangère d'une société primitive," *Ethnies* 19, no. 33–34 (Winter 2009): 114–30.

27. Ibid., 129–30.

28. Ibid., 130.

29. Koran 9:5 explicitly orders that pagans be put to death. Note that this verse belongs to sūra 9, that of *tawba* or repentance, much beloved of bellicose fundamentalists.

30. M. M. Tahā, *Ar-Risāla ath-Thāniya min al-Islām*, 6th ed. (N.p., 1986).

31. See Koran 3:67.

32. Pascal, *Pensées*, intro. T. S. Eliot (New York: Dutton, 1958), nos. 268–70, 77.

33. My emphasis.

34. Tahā, *Ar-Risāla*, 108–9.

35. Cuypers's book, *Le Festin*, was named the international book of the year by the Islamic Republic of Iran, which considered it "one of the best new works in the field of Islamic studies." The award ceremony took place in Tehran, February 7, 2009.

36. This is developed in the epilogue.

37. Koran 26:224–26.


3. ON THE ARAB DECLINE

1. United Nations Human Development Programme, *Arab Human Development Report* (2002). This report was designed and written by Arab academics. See: http://www.arab-hdr.org/publications/other /ahdr/ahdr2002e.pdf

2. For a study of the origins and effects of this movement, see Hamadi Redissi, *Le Pacte de Nadjd* (Paris: Seuil, 2007).

3. See next chapter.

4. "To compose in algebraic calculus . . . a concise book . . . that people will necessarily refer to when establishing their inheritance, legacies, dividing up and arbitration." Al-Khwārizmī, *Le Commencement de l'algèbre*, ed. and trans. Roshdi Rashed (Paris: Albert Blanchard, 2007).

5. Among recent publications in French on this topic, see Hāfez de Chiraz, *Le Dīvān*, ed. and trans. Charles-Henri de Fouchécourt (Lagrasse: Verdier, 2006); Mary Bonnaud, *La Poésie bachique d'Abū Nuwās. Signifiance et symbolique initiatique* (Pessac: Presses universitaires de Bordeaux, 2008); François Clément, ed., *Les Vins d'Orient* (Nantes: Editions du Temps, 2008).

6. Ernest Renan, *Qu'est-ce qu'une nation?* (Paris: Imprimerie nationale, 1996), 240. Bilingual French-English edition, *Qu'est-ce qu'une nation? What Is a Nation?* trans. Wanda Romer Taylor (Toronto: Tapir Press, 1996).

7. Albert Camus, *Actuelles III. Chroniques algériennes, 1939–1958* (Paris: Gallimard, n.d.), 150–51.

8. Jacques Ellul, "Le *dhimmi*: l'opprimé de l'islam," in *Israël. Chance de civilisation* (Paris: Première Partie Editions, 2008), 145–47.

9. Pascal Crozet, *Transfer et appropriation des sciences modernes. L'Exemple égyptien, 1805–1902* (Paris: Guethner, 2009).

10. This manuscript was published by Muhsin Mahdi (Leyden: E. J. Brill, 1986).

## 4. CIVILIZATION OR EXTINCTION

1. See how a Malikite manual from the tenth century deals with this subject, the *Risāla*, by Qayrawāni, chapter 30, "De la guerre sainte," trans. Léon Bercher, bilingual ed. (Algiers: n.p., 1952), 163–66. For an overall look at the notion of *jihād* (whereby we can conclude its inappropriateness to the fundamentalists' current use of the term), see the articles of Hervé Bleuchot, "Le *jihād* et les valeurs universelles," in *Annuaire de l'Afrique du Nord* 33 (Paris: CNRS, 1994), 25–35; and "Le but du *jihād* et son evolution en droit musulman (rite malékite)," in *Revue Maghreb-Europe* (Rabat: Editions de la Porte, 1997–98), 9–31.

2. Ibn Khaldūn, *Le Livre des exemples* I, *Autobiographie, Muquaddima*, trans. A. Cheddadi (Paris: Gallimard, Bibliothèque de la Pléiade, 2002).

3. Henri Pirenne, *Mahomet et Charlemagne* (Paris: Félix Alcan, 1937). Here are two samples of the author's strong views on the subject: "Whereas the Germanic peoples had nothing with which to counter the Christianizing force of the Empire, the Arabs were exalted by a new faith. It was this and this alone that rendered them impossible to integrate" (130); "Islam shattered the Mediterranean unity that the Germanic invasions had allowed to subsist. This is the most essential event to have taken place in European history since the Punic Wars. It marked the end of Antiquity and the start of the Middle Ages" (143). In English, Henri Pirenne, *Mohammed and Charlemagne* (New York: Dover, 2001).

4. Maurice Lombard, *L'Islam dans sa première grandeur, VIIe–Xe siècle* (Paris: Flammarion, 1971). The book concludes thus: "Between China, India, Byzantium and the medieval barbarisms—Turkish, Black African, Western—of late Antiquity and early modernity,

Muslim civilization in its early grandeur was the chronological and geographic crucible, a point of intersection, a vast juncture, an incredible meeting point" (259).

5. Michel Ecochard, *Filiation de monuments grecs, byzantins et islamiques. Une question de géométrie* (Paris: Geuthner, 1977).

6. See my *Face à l'Islam* (Paris: Textuel, 2004), 143–45.

7. Edgar Quinet, *Je sens brûler le nom d'Allah. Voyage à Grenade, Cordoue, Séville* (Montpellier: L'Archange Minotaure, 2001), 69.

8. Rainer Maria Rilke, letter dated December 4, 1912, in *Correspondance avec Marie de la Tour et Taxis* (Paris: Albin Michel, 1960), 122. In English, *Letters of Rainer Maria Rilke, 1910–1926*, trans. Jane Bannard Greene and M. D. Herter Norton (New York: W.W. Norton, 1969). In my *Phantasia*, I also denounce this intrusion in my description of the monument. (Paris: Points, 2004), 121–23.

9. "Beautiful palm! Thou art, like me, a stranger in these places."

10. Henri Stern, *Les Mosaïques de la grande mosquée de Cordoue* (Berlin: Walter de Gruyter, 1976).

11. Giueseppe Michele Crepaldi, *La reale chiesa di San Lorenzo in Torino* (Turin: Rotocalco Dagnino, 1963). This monograph says nothing about the analogy of the cupolas of this church with the mosque of Cordova, but is worth consulting for the planimetrics and cross-section of the church that clearly displays the similarity with the monument of Cordova, as do two photographs (plates 33 and 38), confirming what I was able to observe in situ.

12. Friedrich Nietzsche, *The Antichrist* (New York: Arno, 1972).

13. See the book written by Jean Gallotti at the prompting of Hubert Lyautey: *La Maison et le jardin arabes au Maroc* (Paris: Albert Lévy, 1926; repr., Arles: Actes Sud, 2007). See also the numerous, abundantly illustrated books by Jacques Revault (along with other researchers), devoted to palaces, houses, and dwellings in Tunis, Cairo, and Fez, all published by CNRS editions.

14. Ibn Hazm, *The Ring of the Dove*, trans. A. J. Arberry (London: Luzac, 1953).

15. Ibn Luyūn, *Tratado de agricultura*, trans. and ed. J. Eguaras Ibanez (Grenada: n.p., 1988).

16. Ibn al-'Awwām, *Le Livre de l'agriculture*, trans. J.-J. Clément-Mullet, ed. Mohammed El Faiz (Paris: Sindbad, 2000).

17. Maqrīzī, *Khitat*, vol. 3 (Cairo: Madbūli, 1998), 320.

18. Alexandre Papadopoulo, *L'Islam et l'Art musulman* (Paris: Citadelles et Mazenod, 1976), 278–79.

19. Abū al-Wafā' al-Buzjāni, *Kitāb fī mā yahtāju aç-çāni' min al-a'māl al-handasiyya*, cited by Boris A. Rosenfeld and Adolf P. Youschkevitch, "Géométrie," in *Histoire des sciences arabes*, vol. 2, ed. Roshdi Rashed (Paris: Seuil, 1997), 129.

20. Ibn al-Haytham was well-known enough in Europe to figure in *Le Roman de la Rose* as Alhaçan, author of *Le livre des regards* (literal translation of the Arabic title *Kitāb al-Manāzir*), when Nature, in the context of her own self-definition, comes to describe a rainbow as an optical illusion, before shifting to the topic of mirrors. See line 18,038 of Guillaume de Lorris and Jean de Meung, *Le Roman de la Rose*, ed. and trans. into modern French by Armand Strubel (Paris: Livre de Poche, 1992), 938–41. The passages that Ghiberti uses were transcribed from Latin by Vitellion.

21. Ibn al-Haytham, *Kitāb al-Manāzir*, in Kamāl ad-Dīn Abā 'l-Hasan al-Fārisī, *Kitāb tanqīh al-Manāzir li-dhawīy al-abçār wa 'l-baçā'ir*, Mustafā al-Hijāzī (Cairo: Mustafā al-Hijāzī 1984), I, 335–36.

22. *Risāla fī an-nisba al-'adadiyya wa 'l-handasiyya*, 243–57, in *Rasā'il ikhwān aç-Çafā wa Khillān al Wafā* (Beirut: Dār Sādir, 1957).

23. Erwin Panofsky, *Meaning in the Visual Arts* (Chicago: University of Chicago Press, 1983).

24. Gérard Simon, *L'Archéologie de la vision* (Paris: Seuil, 2003); Erwin Panofsky, *Perspective as Symbolic Form*, trans. Christopher S. Wood (Cambridge, Mass.: Zone Books, 1997).

25. Hans Belting, *Florenz und Bagdad. Eine westöstliche Geschichte des Blicks* (Munich: Verlag C. H. Beck, 2008).

26. Ibn al-Haytham, *Al-Shukūk 'alā Bat'lamyūs* [Dubitationes in Ptolemaeus] (Cairo: A. Sabra and N. Shenaby, 1971).

27. *Institut für Geschichte der Arabisch-Islamischen Wissenschaften* in Frankfurt, Germany.

28. Located in one of the side altars of the Church of Santa Maria Novella in Florence, dated 1428.

29. Rashed, *Histoire des sciences arabes*.

30. See the work of Karine Chemla, notably her articles, "De la synthèse comme moment dans l'histoire des mathématiques," *Diogène* 160 (October–December 1992): 97–114; and "Similarities be-

tween Chinese and Arabic Mathematical Writings: Root Extraction," *Arabic Sciences and Philosophy* 4, no. 2 (1994): 207–66.

31. I am drawing here on material from Roshdi Rashed's translation of Al-Khwārizmī, *Le Commencement de l'algèbre* (Paris: Albert Blanchard, 2007).

32. Ibid., 18.

33. Ibid., 22.

34. The word "algebra" is a Latinized version of the Arabic *al-Jabr*, meaning completion or restoration.

35. See André Allard, "L'Influence des mathématiques arabes dans l'Occident médiéval," in Rashed, *Histoire des sciences arabes* 2, 198–229.

36. Apart from books and articles by Roshdi Rashed, see the study by Philippe Abtral, "La recherche des traditions mathématiques, de l'antiquité hellénistique à l'âge classique en Europe," *Bulletin d'études orientales* 50 (1998): 19–28.

37. Christian Houzel, "Sharaf al-Dīn al-Tūsī et le polygone de Newton," *Arabic Sciences and Philosophy* 5 (1995): 239–262.

38. Miguel Asín Palacios, *L'Islam christianisé. Étude sur le soufisme à travers l'œuvre d'Ibn 'Arabi de Murcie*, trans. B. Dubant (Paris: Éditions de la Maisnie, 1982).

39. A. E. Affifi, *The Mystical Philosophy of Muhid Din Ibnul Arabi* (Cambridge: Cambridge University Press, 1938).

40. Henry Corbin, *Alone with the Alone: Creative Imagination in the Sufism of Ibn 'Arabi* (Princeton, N.J.: Bollingen Paperbacks, 1998).

41. Toshihiko Izutsu, *Sufism and Taoism: A Comparative Study of Key Philosophical Concepts: Ibn 'Arabī, Lao-Tzu and Chuang-Tzu* (Tokyo: n.p., 1983). See also Sachiko Murata, *The Tao of Islam: A Sourcebook on Gender Relationships in Islamic Thought* (Albany: State University of New York Press, 1992).

42. Philo, *De postertiate Caini*, 14–15, trans. R. Arnaldez (Paris: Éditions du Cerf, 1972), 53–55.

43. John Chrysostom, *On the Incomprehensible Nature of God*, trans. Paul W. Harkins (Washington, D.C.: Catholic University of America Press, 1984).

44. Gregory of Nyssa, *The Life of Moses*, trans., intro, and notes, Abraham J. Malherbe and Everett Ferguson (New York: Paulist Press, 1978).

45. Qushayri, *Latā'if al-Ishārāt* [Subtleties of Allusions], vol. 1 (Cairo: I. Basyūni, 1981), 565–67.

46. Asín Palacios, *L'Islam christianisé*, 160–61, 169 for proximity to John of the Cross; 205–6 for similarities with Theresa of Avila; 199 for Ibn 'Arabī's highly accurate knowledge of Plotinus.

47. Ibid., chapter 10, "L'intuition mystique," 163–69.

48. Ibid, 169.

49. Ibn 'Arabī, *L'Interprète des desirs*. (Paris: Albin Michel, 1996).

50. It is these two authors that I identify as the spiritual fathers of my own creative and intellectual process, under the aegis of what I call my double genealogy, Europe and Islam. And this reference to *arche* (ἀρχή) does not imply a conservative approach; on the contrary, I am always striving to keep alive a rapport with the minds of bygone eras, while daring to venture into the new territory available to those who are willing to wander. Did Joyce not call upon the Florentine poet by the familiar "*il padre Dante*"? For resonances between Dante and Ibn 'Arabī, see Miguel Askn Palacios, *L'Eschatologie musulmane dans "La Divine Comédie,"* trans. B. Dubant (Milan: Arche, 1992). See also A. Meddeb, "Le palimpseste du bilingue, Ibn 'Arabī/Dante," in *Du bilinguisme* (Paris: Denoël, 1985), 125–44.

51. See Ramon Menedez Pidal, *Poesia arabe y poesia europea* (Madrid: Espasa-Calpe, 1963).

52. André Miquel and Percy Kemp, *Majnūn et Layla. L'amour fou* (Paris: Sindbad, 1984).

53. Dominique Jullien, *Proust et ses modèles, "Les Mille et Une Nuits" et les "Mémoires" de Saint-Simon* (Paris: José Corti, 1989); see also by the same author, *Les Amoureux de Schéhérazade. Variations modernes sur les Mille et Une Nuits* (Geneva: Droz, 2009). For an approach to French letters through the Arab lens, see A. Meddeb, "La double généalogie à l'épreuve de la langue française," in *Histoire de l'islam et des musulmans en France*, ed. M. Arkoun (Paris: Albin Michel, 2006), 1147–63.

54. A. Meddeb, "L'esprit des *Mille et Une Nuits*," *Théâtre au cinéma* 14 (2003).

55. Alain de Libera, *Penser le Moyen Âge* (Paris: Seuil, 1991). See also Maurice-Ruben Hayoun and Alain de Libera, *Averroès et l'averroïsme* (Paris: PUF, 1991).

56. In his work on political philosophy, Leo Strauss reflects on his century, situating Fārābī among his de rigueur references, after Plato and Aristotle, and before Yehuda Halevi, Maimonides, Machiavelli, Bodin, Spinoza, Locke, Hobbes, Condorcet, etc. See the presence of Fārābī in Leo Strauss, *Persecution and the Art of Writing* (Glencoe, Ill.: Free Press, 1952).

57. See Josef van Ess, *Prémices de la théologie musulmane* (Paris: Albin Michel, 2002).

58. Moshe Ibn 'Ezra, *Kitāb al-Muhādara wal-Mudākara* I [The Book of Conferences and Debates], ed. and trans. Monserrat Abumalhan Mas (Madrid: Consejo Superior de Investigaciones científicas, Instituto de Filología, 1985), 32.

59. Ibid., 30, 152.

60. Ibid., 45.

61. He designates the Koran by the expression *Qur'ān al'Arab* (the Koran of the Arabs), see notably ibid., 103. He often calls the Bible *Kitābuna al-Muqaddas* or "Our Holy Book." See ibid., 125.

62. Designated either by the same term as that used by Muslims to refer to their own traditional authorities (*salaf*, literally "those who came before," meaning "the Elders") or by *Hukama' millatunā*, or "the Wise Men of Our Community."

63. Régis Morélon, "L'astronomie arabe orientale (VIIIe–XIe siècle)," *Histoire des sciences arabes* I (1991):, 66–67.

64. Abū Rayhān Muhammad ibn Ahmad al-Birūnī, *Kitāb fi Tahqīq mā li'l-Hind* (Hyderabad: n.p., 1958), 18–19; English translation by Edward C. Sachau, titled *Alberuni's India* (London: Trübner, 1888), 24–25.

65. Ibid.

66. Pierre Larousse knew that the French word *sofa* derives from this etymology, and says as much in his *Grand Dictionnaire Universel du XIXe siècle* (1876), in the entry devoted to this term, specifying that the name of this piece of furniture comes via Turkish from Arabic, where it designates the bench in Medina, and he was also aware of its purported link to Sufism.

67. For a summary of the conventional etymology of the word, see Kalabādhī (tenth c.), *Traité de soufisme. Les maîtres et les étapes*, trans. R. Deladrière (Paris: Sindbad, 1981), 25–31, with a synthesis on p. 29.

68. Aristotle, *Poetics*, trans. S. H. Butcher (New York: Hill and Wang, 1961).

69. Aristotle, *Of Generation and Corruption*, in *The Basic Works of Aristotle*, ed. Richard McKeon (New York: Random House, 1941).

70. The Dantesque metaphor (*selva oscura*) is nicely adapted to Islam in Louis Aragon's *Le Fou d'Elsa* (Paris: Gallimard, 1963), 14.

71. Ibn Taymiyyah, *Majmū'at ar-Rasā'il wa 'l-Masā'il*, 4 volumes, annotated and commented by Muhammad Rashīd Rizā, Lajnat at-Turāth al-'Arabī (Cairo: Matba'at al-Manār, 1922).,

72. Leo Strauss, "On German Nihilism," *Interpretation* 26, no. 3 (1999).

73. Oswald Spengler, *The Decline of the West*, trans. Arthur Helps and Charles Francis Atkinson (New York: Oxford University Press, 1991); Carl Schmitt, *The Crisis of Parliamentary Democracy*, trans. Ellen Kennedy (Cambridge, Mass.: MIT Press, 1985).

74. The expression is Thomas Mann's, in 1922, with regard to a book by Spengler.

75. Already, Simone Weil paid homage to "the French . . . lovers of Arab culture" who form a "milieu" and who "are starting to constitute a source of renewal for French culture." See *Écrits historiques et politiques* (Paris: Gallimard, 1960), 365.

76. Johann Wolfgang von Goethe, *West-Eastern Divan*, trans. Edward Dowden (London: J. M. Dent and Sons, 1914).

77. A. Meddeb, *La Maladie de l'Islam* (Paris: Seuil, 2002), 79–81.

78. Bernard Lewis, *What Went Wrong? Western Impact and Middle Eastern Response* (New York: Oxford University Press, 2001).

79. Al-Jāhiz, *Kitāb al-Hayawān*, vol. 1 (Cairo: A. S. Hārūn, 1938), 55–58.

80. Melhen Chokr, *Zandaqa et zindīq en islam au second siècle de l'hégire* (Damascus: Institut français de Damas, 1993), 66–68.

81. Ibid., 66.

82. Its need as link between subject and predicate was formulated for the first time two centuries earlier, in the tenth century, by Fārābī in a language, Arabic, that does not have the verb "to be"! See his book on logic, *Kitāb al-Hurūf* (Beirut: Muhsin Mahdi, 1986), 111–13.

## 5. ENLIGHTENMENT BETWEEN HIGH
## AND LOW VOLTAGE

1. 'Abd Allah Ibn al-Muqaffa', *Kalila and Dimna; or the Fables of Bidpai*, trans. Wyndham Knatchbull (Oxford: W. Baxter, 1819).

2. *Mulhid* means "he who diverges from the straight path," which went on to designate atheists in the ninth century.

3. Dominique Urvoy, *Les Penseurs libres dans l'Islam classique* (Paris: Albin Michel, 1996), 40.

4. The inquisition is called *mihna* in Arabic, literally, a trial or ordeal. See the article that M. Hinds devotes to this term in the *Encyclopédie de l'Islam*, vol. 7 (Leiden: E. J. Brill, 1993), 2–6.

5. As Dominique Urvoy calls them.

6. Abū Hātim, a Shiite theologian and Ismaili preacher.

7. Abū Hātim Rāzī, *Kitāb al 'Alām an-Nubuwwa* [The Book of Prophetic Signs] (Tehran: S. as-Sawy and G. R. Aavani, 1977). See also F. Brion, who translates and analyzes passages reporting the statements that Abū Hātim Rāzī puts in the mouth of Abū Bakr Rāzī, in "Philosophie et Révélation: traduction annotée de six extraits du *Kitāb al 'Alām an-Nubuwwa* d' Abū Hātim Rāzī," *Bulletin de philosophie médiévale* 28 (1986): 135–62.

8. Ibn Khaldūn, *Le Livre des exemples*.

9. Here, the Algazal of the Latins, famous in Europe for his work *The Incoherence of the Philosophers* (*Tahāfut al-Falāsifa*), which provoked a response from Averroes a century later, *The Incoherence of the Incoherence* (*Tahāfut al-Tahāfut*).

10. The exhibit I designed and directed in Barcelona (May 26–September 25, 2005) provides a demonstration of this Islamic "Occidentalism." See A. Meddeb, *Occident vist des d'Orient* (The West Seen from the East] (Barcelona: CCCB, 2005).

11. Goethe and Heine both acknowledge their debt to Spinoza.

12. In Muslim law, this was called *bid'a hasana* (good innovation), *mahmūda* (praiseworthy), *mandūba* (recommended), *mubāha* (authorized).

13. Quoted by Ignaz Goldziher, *Le Dogme et la Loi en Islam* (Paris: L'éclat/Geuthner, 2005), 217.

14. Hamdan Khodja, *Le Miroir* (Paris: Sindbad, 1985), 37–38.

15. A. Meddeb, ed., "Postcolonialisme," special issue, *Dédale* 5–6 (Spring 1997): 12.

16. Ali Abderraziq, *L'Islam et les fondements du pouvoir*, trans. Abdou Filali-Ansary (Paris: La Découverte, 1994).

17. Taha Hussayn, *Fī 'l-Adab al-Jāhilī* [On Pre-Islamic Literature], 10th ed. (Cairo: Dār al-Ma'ārif, 1969).

18. Taha Hussayn, *Mustaqbal ath-Thaqāfa fī Miçr* [The Future of Culture in Egypt] (Cairo, 1939).

19. I say "practically irreversible" to temper any absolute judgment, and as a reminder that history shows that nothing is ever a definitive gain: Enlightenment values have come under attack in the very place of their birth and could not prevent Europe from experiencing the bleakest period of its existence, with totalitarianism, national socialism, and Stalinism.

20. In ancient times, and in very different contexts of metaphysics and religion, far from secular reason. The cult of fire established by Zoroaster, the Platonist duality of the brightness of ideas versus the darkness of the cave, the Manichaean duality of good associated with day and evil with night, the resurgence of the metaphysics of *Ishrāq*, illuminism reinvented by Sohrawardi (1155–91), which combines the metaphors of Zoroaster, Plato, and Mani with the Koranic verse of Light ("Light upon Light . . . ," Koran 24:35), to situate the glow of dawn in the east of its origin where the soul will one day return, as opposed to the west as end point, prison of the body, the condition of Man in his earthly abode. See A. Meddeb, *L'Exil occidental* (Paris: Albin Michel, 2005), 57–58.

21. What jurists called *bid'a sayyi'a* (evil innovation), *madhmūna* (blameworthy), *muharrama* (prohibited), *makrūha* (reprobate).

22. Leo Strauss, *Jewish Philosophy and the Crisis of Modernity: Essays and Lectures in Modern Jewish Thought* (Albany: State University of New York Press, 2012). See chapter 7: "Why We Remain Jews" (1962).

23. The expression is credited to Henri Michaux.

24. Pascal, *Pensées* (New York: E. P. Dutton, 1958), no. 434.

25. For more on this topic, see A. Meddeb, *The Malady of Islam*, (New York: Basic Books, 2003).

26. Jacques Derrida and Jürgen Habermas, *Philosophy in a Time of Terror: Dialogues with Jurgen Habermas and Jacques Derrida, Interviewed by Giovanna Borradori* (Chicago: University of Chicago Press, 2003).

## 6. THE PHYSICS AND METAPHYSICS OF NATURE

1. See the article that Morgan Guiraud devotes to it in the *Dictionnaire du Coran*, ed. Mohammed Ali Amir-Moezzi (Paris: Robert Laffont, 2007), 114–19.

2. *Les Penseurs grecs avant Socrate. De Thalès de Milet à Prodicos*, trans., intro., and notes Jean Voilquin (Paris: GF-Flammarion, 1964), 47.

3. Karl Wittfogel, *Oriental Despotism: A Comparative Study of Total Power* (New York: Vintage, 1981).

4. See Mohammed El Faiz's studies on hydraulic engineering between Seville and Marrakesh during the Almohad era (twelfth–thirteenth c.) and beyond. All this author's works are published with Actes Sud: *Jardins de Marrakech* (2000); *Marrakech* (2000); *Les Maîtres de l'eau. Histoire de l'hydraulique arabe* (2005).

5. Louis Massignon, "Enquête sur les corporations musulmanes d'artisans et de commerçants," *Revue du monde musulman* 58 (1924).

6. As did Raymond Lull, who found fault with the Muslims' sensual paradise that would reek of excrement. Here is what the Gentile argued to the Saracen with regard to an Eden of the senses: "If things are as you say, then there must be filth in Paradise, for according to the natural order of things, from a man who eats and drinks and lies with women there must come forth filth and corruption, which filth is an ugly thing to see and touch and smell, and to talk about." Ramon Llull, *Selected Works of Ramon Llull* trans., ed. Anthony Bonner (Princeton: Princeton University Press, 1985) 291.

7. *Al-Andalus. Anthologie*, trans. Brigitte Foulon, Emmanuelle Tixier du Mesnil (Paris: Flammarion, 2009) 295–302.

8. Ibid., 293–94 (author's translation).

9. The most famous work in this area was that of Seville-born Ibn al-'Awwām, *Le Livre de l'agriculture* (*Kitāb al-Filāha*), translated from Arabic into French by J.-J. Clement-Mullet, ed. Mohammed El Faiz (Paris: Sindbad, 2000), 84.

10. Manuscript that dates back to Hijrī 740 (1348), conserved in Grenada, Escuela de Estudios Arabes, inventory number GR-E Ara ms. vol. 14 (ant.A-5, 14): Ibn Luyūn, *Tratado de agricultura*, trans. and ed. J. Eguaras Ibanez (Grenada: n.p., 1988), 84.

11. *Jeune homme au brin de narcisse*, Iran, mid–sixteenth century; gouache, ink, and gold on paper, 14.5 × 8.3 cm, Louvre Museum, acquisition 1916, bequest G. Marteau.

12. A. Meddeb, "La trace, le signe," in *L'Image dans le monde arabe*, ed. G. Beaugé and J.-F. Clément (Paris: CNRS, 1995), 107–23.

13. In Arabic: *Kun fa yakūn.*

14. Ibn 'Arabī, *Al-Futūhāt al-Makkiyya*, vol. 2 (Cairo: N.p, n.d.), chapter 198:12, 427–29.

15. Koran 2:30, 38:26.

16. Baltasar Gracián, *The Critick*, trans. Sir Paul Rycaut (London: Printed by T. N. for Henry Brome, 1681). Oddly enough, Pelegrin says not a word about the Arab descent of the Spanish novel. Eurenio d'Ors, on the other hand, addresses the issue in "L'autodidacte de Gracian," in *Du baroque*, trans. Agathe Rouart-Valéry (Paris: Gallimard, 1968), 39–44.

17. Ibn Tufayl, *Hayy Ibn Yaqzān* (Beirut: Dār al-Mashriq, 1986), 77–78. See also Ibn Tufayl, *Le Philosophe sans maître* (*Histoire de Hayy Ibn Yaqzān*), trans. Léon Gauthier (Algiers: SNED, 1969), 109–11.

18. *L'Agriculture nabatéenne*, 3 vols., Arabic translation attributed to Ibn Wahshiyya (tenth c.), critical ed. Toufic Fahd (Damascus: Institut français de Damas, 1998).

19. Ibn al-Baytar, *Traité des simples*, 3 vols., trans. Lucien Leclerc (Paris: Institut du monde arabe, 1987).

20. Koran 30:30.

21. See the article that Genviève Gobillot devotes to this notion, in her entry titled "Nature innée" in Amir-Moezzi, *Dictionnaire du Coran*, 591–95.

22. *Le Calendrier de Cordoue*, written in 961, bringing together works attributed to 'Arīb ibn S'ad and to the bishop Recemundo, translated from Arabic and annotated by Charles Pellat (Leiden: E. J. Brill, 1961).

23. The famous line from Ibn Khaldūn that I have just quoted originates in a passage that evokes the effects of this nomad invasion. See *Muqaddima*, in particular chapter 25 of the second part of book 1, eloquently titled "Lands Conquered by the Arabs Will Soon Fall to Ruin." Ibn Khaldūn, *The Muqaddimah*, trans. Franz Rosenthal (Princeton, N.J.: Princeton University Press, 1967).

24. Which was so important in renewing the self-concern so typical of Arabs of ages past.

EPILOGUE: RELIGION AND COSMOPOLITICS

1. Immanuel Kant, *Toward Perpetual Peace and Other Writings on Politics, Peace and History*, trans. David L. Colclasure, ed. Pauline Kleingeld (New Haven, Conn.: Yale University Press, 2006).

2. Nicolaus of Cusa, *Toward a New Council of Florence: "On the Peace of Faith" and Other Works by Nicolaus of Cusa*, trans. and intro. William F. Wertz Jr. (Washington, D.C.: Schiller Institute, 1993). But at the very end of his work, Nicolaus of Cusa is the first to use the expression "perpetual peace."

3. Kant, *Toward Perpetual Peace.*

4. Nicolaus of Cusa, *Toward a New Council of Florence.*

5. This is the strategy deployed by Louis Massignon as a Catholic grappling with Islam. And it would appear to be the one that inspired European Catholics living in Cairo within the community housed by the Dominican convent situated in the 'Abbasiyya quarter.

6. Nicolaus of Cusa, *Toward a New Council of Florence.*

7. Moshe Ibn 'Ezra, *Kitāb al-Muhādara wal-Mudākara*, I [The Book of Conferences and Debates], ed. and trans. Monserrat Abumalhan Mas (Madrid: Consejo Superior de Investigaciones cientificas, Instituto de Filologia, 1985), 128 (among others), where he cites the second and third to the last verses of the sūra "The Poets" (Koran 26:225–26).

8. Ibn 'Ezra, *Kitāb al-Muhādara wal-Mudākara*, 20–21.

9. Known by the name El-Naguid Rabbi Samuel, transcribed in Hebrew characters within a text in Arabic lettering. For more on this, see ibid., 66–73.

10. Such at least is the opinion of Maria-Rosa Menocal in *L'Andalousie arabe, une culture de la tolerance, VIIe–XVe siècle* (Paris: Autrement, 2003).

11. Roger Arnaldez, "Controverse d'Ibn Hazm contre Ibn Nagrila le juif," *Revue des mondes musulmans et de la Méditerranée* 13, no. 13–14 (1973): 41–48.

12. See what I have said in this regard in *Sortir de la malediction* (Paris: Seuil, 2008), 248–51.

13. Ibn Arabī, *Fuçūç al-Hikam* I (Cairo: Abū al 'Alā 'Affīfī, 1946), 72.

14. Ibid., I, 226.

15. Ibn 'Ezra, *Kitāb al-Muhādara wal-Mudākara*, 72.

16. Cited by Hervé Pasqua in the introduction to his French translation of Nicolaus of Cusa's *On the Peace of Faith*. See Nicolas de Cues, *La Paix de la foi*, trans. and intro. Hervé Pasqua (Paris: Pierre Téqui, 2008), 64–65.

17. Not unlike that proposed by Pascal in his *Pensées* (New York: E. P. Dutton, 1958), no. 698.

18. My own ancestors were victims of this purge.

19. This acknowledgment is the precondition for a just criticism of Israel when this country acts as a state blinded by its own power, as was the case in Gaza (December 2008–January 2009). See A. Meddeb, "Pornographie de l'horreur," *Le Monde*, January 12, 2009; A. Meddeb and B. Stora, "Au-delà de Gaza," *Le Monde*, February 26, 2009.

20. Alexis de Tocqueville, *Sur l'Algérie* (Paris: G-F Flammarion, 2003), 197–98. The observation is extracted from the 1847 report.

21. See "La dernière république," in *Amnistier l'Apartheid. Travaux de la Commission Vérité et Réconciliation*, dir. Desmond Tutu, ed. Philippe-Joseph Salazar (Paris: Seuil, 2004). See also Barbara Cassin, Olivier Cayla, and Philippe-Joseph Salazar, eds., *Vérité, Réconciliation, Réparation*, Le Genre Humain 43 (Paris: Seuil, 2004). For the complete *Truth and Reconciliation Commission of South Africa Report* in English, see South African Government Information, March 21, 2003, http://www.info.gov.za/otherdocs/2003/trc/.

22. Barack Obama, *Dreams of My Father* (New York: Crown, 2007).

## APPENDIX A. THE VEIL UNVEILED: DIALOGUE WITH CHRISTIAN JAMBET

Transcription of a radio program I host, *Cultures d'Islam*, broadcast by France Culture on January 25, 2004. A first version of this text was published in *Esprit* no. 305 (June 2004): 131–47.

1. Koran 33:53, 42:51.

2. See A. Meddeb, *Les Dits de Bistami* (Paris: Fayard, 1989).

3. Ibid., fragment 328.

4. Ibid., fragments 26, 181.

5. Ibid., fragment 372.

6. Translated into French as *Somme spirituelle* (Paris: Sindbad, 1986).

7. Meddeb, *Les Dits de Bistāmi*, fragment 382.

8. Henry Corbin, *Creative Imagination in the Sufism of Ibn Arabi*, trans. Ralph Manheim (Princeton, N.J.: Princeton University Press, 1969).

9. Ibn ʿArabī, *L'Interprète des desires*, trans. Maurice Gloton (Paris: Albin Michel, 1996). Ibn ʿArabī, *Tarjumān al-Ashwāq*, trans. Reynold A. Nicholson (London: Theosophical Publishing House, 1911).

APPENDIX B. OBAMA IN CAIRO

A slightly different version of this text appeared under the title "Barack Hussein Obama, merci!" *Esprit*, no. 356 (July 2009): 6–9.